$\mathcal{B}c$

The IRA Survival Guide

How to Manage Your IRA for Maximum Benefits Under the New Tax Law

David M. Brownstone

amacom

American Management Association

*This book is available at a special
discount when ordered in bulk quantities.
For information, contact Special Sales Department,
AMACOM, a division of American Management Association,
135 West 50th Street, New York, NY 10020.*

Library of Congress Cataloging-in-Publication Data

Brownstone, David M.
    The IRA survival guide.

    Includes index.
    1. Individual retirement accounts--United States.
I. American Management Association.   II. Title.
HG1660.U5B76 1987   332.024'01   86-47806
ISBN 0-8144-5861-0

Printing number

10 9 8 7 6 5 4 3 2 1

Preface

As IRA funds have grown, so has the need for a clear, simple work that outlines, explains, and compares all the main investments possible and appropriate for IRAs, taking into account the special features and tax advantages unique to IRAs. This book responds to that need, and goes further, by also fitting IRA investment strategies into the context of lifetime financial planning. Please note that this work reflects the changes embodied in the 1986 tax law.

My thanks to Irene M. Franck, whose major developmental contributions as always have shaped and greatly improved the work; to Jacques Sartisky, for his ever-helpful financial insights; to Gene Hawes, who has once again endured and perhaps sometimes even enjoyed much of the discussion preceding the writing of the work; to our co-workers, Mary Racette and Mary Bunch, who have typed and copyread the book; and to our editor and publisher, Peter H. Shriver and Robert A. Kaplan, who have been so helpful all along the way.

David M. Brownstone
Chappaqua, New York, 1986

Contents

1

Seeing Your IRA as a Lifelong Investment Opportunity

Every once in a while, something comes along that can change the entire personal financial planning picture for millions of us. The advent of Social Security in the 1930s was such an event, for it provided a basic government-guaranteed later-years income for the first time. The tax-advantaged company pension plan was another, for it added very substantial company-guaranteed later-years income promises to Social Security and other government-guaranteed pensions.

In recent years, another such major form has emerged, this one far more capable of being directly controlled by people doing their own sound long-term financial planning. It is the Individual Retirement Account (IRA), which makes it possible for individuals to build a very significant long-term tax-advantaged stake of their own, independent of Social Security and company pension plans. Tens of millions of

Americans have started to do just that, with some already beginning to develop and manage quite substantial IRA funds. How to manage those funds well—meaning at most profit and with least associated risk—is what this book is about.

It may be more important to manage these IRA funds well and safely than many of us yet realize. Economic circumstances, and with them government's and business's ability and willingness to keep promises, have changed greatly in the last decade. The truth is that far more of us are living far longer than anyone anticipated when pension promises were made. The truth is also that, as a country, we are not as rich as we thought we were when those promises were being made.

In the altered circumstances created by the convergence of those two truths, the federal government has begun the long process of whittling away at promised Social Security benefits, and companies all over the country are both cutting back on pension promises and seriously compromising the integrity of pension funds. Those IRA and other portable personal pension plan funds we are now creating will, for many of us, in the long run make the difference between decently lived long lives and decades of near-poverty in our later years. They are that important. And managing them well is vital.

Because of the tax advantages involved, IRA funds really do accumulate astonishingly fast, even at the seemingly low levels of contribution allowed by law and even when quite conservatively invested. That basic fact about IRAs continues to be so even after passage of the 1986 tax law. Some people who started early are already managing tens of thousands of dollars in their IRAs, and are well on their way to the long run-up that will result later on in million-dollar IRAs. Yes, inflation must be taken into account, and yes, to some extent the million-dollar IRA is a myth perpetrated by eager investment sellers, intent on getting their share of the multi-billion-dollar IRA investment market. But the million-dollar IRA is not entirely to be discounted, for there is truth here along with the puffery. Because of the tax advantage involved, the IRA allows you to have a fair chance of building a meaningful investment fund that grows considerably faster than the rate of inflation, one worth as much in real dollars as your Social Security or company pension benefits—perhaps even more.

Consider, for example, a working couple who both started IRAs five years ago, and have each put in $2,000 every year since then. Assume that those IRA investment funds have grown and compounded at 10% a year, an entirely rational and conservative expectation in these years. At that rate the $20,000 they invested will have now become almost $27,000. At the same rate of contribution and yield, that IRA fund will be worth almost $1,200,000 35 years out.

But now let us be very realistic, and take inflation into account. Assume you make the same $4,000 yearly family IRA contributions, but assume that in the long term, no matter how skillfully you manage those funds, you succeed in getting an average return of only 4% over the rate of inflation. That is a reasonable long-term expectation: in some low inflation and relatively high yield periods, you may do far better than that, but there will also be years in which you will do well to gain a point or two on inflation. That was so in the double-digit inflation years of the early 1970s, and those times may very well come again during the long periods in which IRA funds are held and developed.

So we are no longer looking at a million-dollar IRA fund, or anything remotely resembling it. Not in real dollars. On the other hand, we *are* looking at a very healthy real-dollar IRA of more than $300,000 the same 35 years out. You will have to pay some taxes on distributions from that fund later on, and at ordinary tax rates, but you are still going to wind up with a later-years fund that will yield yearly income worth at least what your Social Security payments are worth, and probably as much as most company pension payouts as well.

Many people who are now in mid-career will not have as long as 35 years in which to accumulate IRA funds, and their fund buildups will therefore be smaller. They can still be quite significant, though. Only 17 to 18 years out, your $4,000 yearly compounding at 10% becomes about $200,000, which adjusts to a real-dollar $100,000. Those are very significant numbers, however; the difference between making it decently in your later years and not making it can rest on the $5,000 to $10,000 that is generated each year by even this relatively modest IRA fund.

Notably, many IRA funds today are already in the range of $100,000 and more, and are therefore already providing major investment opportunities to their holders. These are the funds—often quite large—that come from rolling over other pension plans into IRAs, as when a job change results in payout of a substantial sum of vested pension plan money. (If not rolled over into an IRA, it would be treated as ordinary income and taxed as a lump sum, therefore at very high rates in the year received, though the new tax law does provide for a mixture of capital gains income averaging techniques that provides a little relief.) More on this in Chapter 3, which is a brief refresher on the basic mechanics of IRAs. Here, it is easy enough to note that someone fortunate to start early with a big rolled-over IRA may later enjoy the fruits of a multi-million-dollar IRA fund, which in today's real dollars may very well be a million-dollar IRA.

Looking at it clearly, you can see that the IRA funds you manage and develop become extraordinarily important to you. They can easily become large enough to supply much of the needed funds for your later years, even after taking inflation into account. And they are yours; no Congress can whittle away at them, as many Congresses will at Social Security during our lifetimes. No company can destroy them, after compromising employee pension funds while defending against corporate raiders, or depleting them while the business is going bad. You own the money in your IRA; it is your own tax-advantaged portable personal pension plan, for you to use and grow as safely and as fast as possible.

Safe and fast: it's the oldest contradiction in the investment game. It is not only a seeming contradiction, either, to be easily put aside after invoking some sort of standard risk-and-reward formula. For there is no such formula, and that is especially so in uncertain times. Even yesterday's blue chip corporate bond may be today's downgraded, rather risky investment, after a corporate raid has sadly depleted corporate assets, for example, or an environmental disaster has brought ruinous lawsuits and adverse judgments.

On the other hand, safety and yield certainly continue to be generally related. A short-term, federally insured certificate of deposit (CD) is generally going to yield less than a riskier, though well-rated, corporate bond, still less than a low-rated junk bond that carries much higher risk. Investment professionals pay a great deal of attention to risk-reward relationships, and thereby much influence the prices and yields of trading securities.

Normally in the investment marketplace, the question of potential reward—that is, yield on investment—is much influenced by tax factors, for the reward that is being measured is *net after-tax yield*, the yield remaining after necessary tax payments have been taken into account. That yield may be a combination of change in market value and dividends, as with a share of stock, or of market value and interest, as with a traded bond. Or it may be measured solely by gain or loss in market value, as with a piece of raw land, or solely by net after-tax interest, as with a bank CD or a municipal bond. Wherever yield is affected by tax factors, it must be adjusted to include taxes before it can be properly perceived. That is axiomatic in the investment world.

But that is precisely the axiom that changes when you are dealing with tax-advantaged IRA funds. For then *the tax aspects do not matter at all*, as all yield is tax-free until distribution years later, when it is all taxable. As a direct result, *the risk-reward question absolutely must be reexamined for every kind of investment before putting IRA money into it*.

For example, a municipal bond or municipal bond fund yielding a nontaxable 8% yearly may seem attractive to someone in a 40% combined federal, state, and city or county tax bracket. For that person the 8% yield would be equivalent to an almost 14% yield from fully taxable investments. (Of course, that 14% yield is likely to be from a far riskier investment than many lower yields; more on that later on, when the specifics of municipals are discussed. But in spite of that risk, many in the high income tax brackets may still buy, for the net yield from the investment is high.)

However, if that same person is looking for an IRA fund investment, the same equivalency tradeoffs no longer apply. Interest earned by bonds or bond funds used as IRAs is not taxed, so it is no longer accurate to say that 8% is "the same as" almost 14%. Thus, for IRA funds, that municipal's 8% yield is likely to be far too low to justify the risks involved. For IRAs, the municipal bond or bond fund yields *only the interest rate*, and must compete with every other kind of investment on that basis. And when you can buy a fully federally insured bond that yields 8%, rather than a risky municipal at 8%, the choice is perfectly clear. In those circumstances, many far safer investments will yield considerably more than the municipals, and be much better IRA investments.

That sort of reexamination of investment opportunities in the light of vastly changed tax considerations is one of the main purposes of this work. People investing their already tax-advantaged IRA money need not worry about tax sheltering that money (although there may still be opportunities that give even better shelter than the IRA, usually at much greater risk). Nor do IRA owners need to worry about such matters as taxes on imputed interest, for IRAs short-circuit these kinds of tax considerations before they arise.

Similarly, the key question of leverage—in essence, the use of borrowed money to try to make money—must be reexamined when considering each kind of investment as a possible IRA vehicle, for IRA rules prohibit the use of borrowed funds. That lets out some kinds of highly speculative investments, such as commodity options, and some ways of making investments more speculative, as when you buy stocks on margin. On the other hand, it also eliminates the use of IRA money for such very sober investments as home purchase, for which almost all home buyers must use mortgage loans.

The fact is that IRA money is very special long-term money, and that all potential IRA investments are best very carefully examined in light of the immense advantages and some potential disadvantages offered by the nature of the IRA itself. That is what this book will do, after some comments on finding sound investment advice and a brief review of IRA rules and mechanics.

Before we go into that brief review, however, there is one approach that needs to be stressed again and again: *No matter how you decide to handle your IRA money at any given time or in any given period, it is essential to know enough to make your own informed decisions as to the investment of that money.* That applies whether you are handling your IRA funds day-to-day, as in the case of a self-directed trading account, or far less frequently, as when you watch your money carefully but make only a few decisions each year about where to place it (for instance, when your IRA money is in mutual funds, bank certificates of deposit, or insurance company annuities). Either way, you should see yourself as fully responsible for handling the financial side of your own life, and should watch your money, keep abreast of financial marketplace matters, and make very sure that you know enough to make the right decisions at the right times. (For a broader-scale approach to effective personal financial planning, which is the essential underpinning of successful long-term IRA development, see my most recent works in this area—*The Manager's Lifelong Money Book*, with Jacques Sartisky, AMACOM, 1986; *Moneywise*, Watts, 1985; *The Saver's Guide to Sound Investing*, Watts, 1985—or any of several other substantial works in the field.)

It is vital to bear in mind, throughout a whole lifetime of saving and investing, that in the long run no one else will watch your money as carefully as you will. It is also vital to understand that those who treat the financial side of life as if it were a real second career, a business to be learned like any other business, will soon enough learn how to manage their own financial health far better than anyone can manage it for them. You will need to seek sound financial advice, but the truth is that no high-powered financial adviser can possibly spend much time with any single small or medium-size investor. You really have no choice but to manage your own financial affairs, if you want them managed well.

The truth is also that today's financial marketplace is full of people holding themselves out as expert advisers on every financial instrument and technique under the sun. What nonsense. It is patently impossible for anyone to keep up on a day-to-day basis with more than a modest fraction of the savings and investment vehicles and techniques available. The truth is also that there are more speculation, conflicts of interest, ineptitude, and outright fraud in the financial marketplace than at any time since just before the great crash of 1929. You had best be extremely skeptical, extremely cautious, and increasingly skilled when it comes to building your IRA and your lifetime financial plan, for there are great hazards out there today.

2
Finding Sound, Current Investment Advice

To develop the investment skills that will enable you to manage and build your IRA—and your other investments—you will need to find sources of sound, current, continuing investment information and advice. You will also need to seek out and consistently use sound people in the financial planning business, for they are there and available, side by side with all those eager sellers. Yes, fraud and ineptitude are out there in the financial marketplace, but that does not mean that it is right to try to go it alone with your investments, or for that matter with your lifelong financial planning, as you continually work out and revise it. All of us can use some skilled help, with both lifetime planning and the current investments that are part of that lifetime planning; this book focuses on the current investment side of the matter.

A disclaimer of sorts is in order here. Although this work has been updated in light of the new tax law, you should not look to a bound book like this one for current, very specific investment advice. This is a book of basic analysis and advice, which takes many months to conceive and write, and then many months more to produce and take to market. Even if you have purchased this book in its first month after publication, the words you are reading were quite likely written a year ago, and then revised in light of then-current circumstances several months ago, which is the author's last chance at it before it goes to press. Even much more quickly produced information annuals, which are revised until very close to press time, are also going to be at least a month or two out of date on publication, and even a month can be a very long time in highly volatile financial markets.

That is why you will find no specific recommendations in this book or in most books like it. Where you do find such recommendations, *mistrust them*, for they are out of date. The author who looks at a steady, stable, Rock of Gibraltar kind of stock like IBM and unhesitatingly recommends it as a good buy is being very foolish indeed, for even that company may encounter the kinds of problems that could depress its stock a year later; you simply cannot know that far in advance. Similarly, and quite obviously, an author looking at an extraordinarily well-performing Magellan or Fidelity fund in early 1986 would be very wrong indeed to recommend purchase of either one, for readers won't see the printed advice until perhaps a year later.

Circumstances change; timing is all. Yesterday's booming mutual fund may be today's leading loser, as so many small investors learned in the early 1970s. For usable insights, you must look to current publications and up-to-date advice from investment advisers who are carefully and skillfully following investment opportunities.

Don't be afraid to spend some information- and advice-gathering money to make money, especially if you are considering moving some of your IRA money beyond the safest, most risk-averse federally insured bank savings accounts out into a wider and perhaps better-yielding investment world. These IRA funds can build very fast and go very high, and serious amounts of money require very serious treatment. If you gain an extra 2% in any year on even a $20,000 IRA fund, you gain $400, which becomes $400 more compounding tax-free in your IRA. An extra 2% on a pension-plan rollover $100,000 fund is $2,000, likewise compounding. On the other side of the coin, the thousands you can lose while following the advice of some eager investment seller may be avoidable, if you are willing to spend some time and money on getting skilled, keeping up, and finding some sound advice.

Publications

Amateur or professional, anyone seeking to make informed investment moves must have a steady flow of good information. You have to keep up, both with the specific investments and kinds of investments you are interested in and with the multiple contexts within which those developments are taking place.

It is foolish to follow the herd, buying whatever is "hot" and trendy at the moment, or to make your specific moves because of what "the market" is doing. It is equally foolish to pay no attention at all to wider trends; for example, you can be reasonably sure that there will in this period be an upward push in stock market levels whenever interest rates trend downward. For some years now, a certain hydraulic tendency has been apparent in this regard, with interest rates and stock prices moving opposite each other.

Yet it would make no sense for a small investor to buy thousands of dollars' worth of current investment services, such as a major brokerage office will have. What does make sense is to find a continuing source for a wide range of general financial and related information, add to that one or more investment advisory publications, learn where to find other information as needed, and locate a sound financial adviser.

The single substantial source shared by almost everyone in the American financial marketplace is the *Wall Street Jour-*

nal. It very reliably supplies a wide range of information on financial matters, on the political and economic contexts within which those matters occur, and on almost all the kinds of investments in which you might put your IRA money. Subscribing to it is worthwhile, whether you are a neophyte or an experienced investor. In a way, it is even more useful for the beginner, for although much will be unfamiliar at first, the very act of consistently reading the newspaper will serve as a powerful self-educator. You do have to *read* it, though, perhaps with an investor's dictionary by your side early on. Leaving a major and vitally important ongoing source of information unused or too lightly used is only fooling yourself.

As your investment funds and investing interests grow, you may well decide to buy other investment newspapers and advisory services, such as *Barron's* weekly investment newspaper, or the rather expensive but very useful Dow Jones, Zweig, Value Line, or other advisory services. You will find them frequently advertised; as soon as you buy your first introductory short-term subscription to any one of them, you will also be mail-solicited endlessly by all the others. That is all to the good; such short-term subscriptions and solicitations can serve to bring you knowledge of many specialized and useful investment advisory services. As of this writing, these services are generally tax-deductible; they are worth having even if the tax law later limits or ends such deductability.

Much of the specific investment information you seek over the years will be as near as the public library. Most large regional libraries and many of their branches will subscribe to a substantial number of expensive investment services and books. There you are quite likely to find any of several basic information services, such as the whole line of Moody's services, including *Moody's Bank and Finance Manual, Bond Record, Bond Survey, Dividend Record, Handbook of Common Stocks, Industrial Manual, Investors' Fact Sheets, Municipal and Government Manual, Over-the-Counter (OTC) Industrial Manual, Public Utility Manual,* and *Transportation Manual.* You may also find the Standard & Poor's reports, many of them covering the same ground, including *Standard & Poor's American Stock Exchange Reports, Bond Guide, Daily Stock Price Record, Dividend Record, Earnings Forecaster, Fixed Income Investor, Industry Surveys, Municipal Bond Selector, Over-the-Counter Stock Reports, Register of Corporations, Directors, and Executives, Standard Corporation Records*, and *Standard New York Stock Exchange Reports*.

You will also find mutual fund information, carried in such large, detailed services as Wiesenberger's *Investment Companies*, and in such books as Hirsch's annual *Mutual Funds Almanac* and the Investment Company Institute's annual *Mutual Fund Fact Book*. A good many of these also include newsletters, and most appear in looseleaf, with quite current material. Together, they supply much of the basic information you will seek on individual investments.

For a wider range of business and financial information sources, consult such works as Brownstone and Carruth's *Where to Find Business Information*, Grant Cote's *Directory of Business and Financial Services*, and Lorna Daniell's *Business Information Sources*. All are standard works, available in most libraries.

In your library you will also be able to consult the reference librarian, and that can mean a great deal to you when seeking information. Most professional reference librarians are extraordinarily well informed, extremely eager to help, and accustomed to reaching through even the most imprecisely formulated queries to understand and properly respond to the real question being asked. And what they don't know, they know how to find out. By all means let your reference librarians help you. If at all possible, though, save your more complex questions for times when they are not being besieged by large numbers of puzzled students and other library users.

Those who can use electronic financial and business databases through business or home computers can very easily find all the above information and a great deal more.

Such massive groups of databases as Dialog and Nexis are really collections of hundreds of major databases, and will supply enormous amounts of information about any widely traded public company. As all the world's major financial and business publications find their way into such databases, and as additional information services are created directly for databases, literally all the information available in the world is becoming accessible directly from your computer screen.

Those who have computers hooked up to such databases in their businesses may be able to gain access to this developing body of information right now. But for most home computer users who are small investors, the cost of such access is, so far, prohibitive. That will change, however, as tens of millions of people in all countries begin to use the massive worldwide information system that is now being born.

Finding Sound Investment Advisers

Your own developing competence in matters financial is your best guarantee that you will be able to find, understand, evaluate, and work with sound financial advisers. Clearly, what you should be seeking is full-scale financial planning advice, of which sound investment advice is part; how you work with your IRA money is only part of your total financial planning picture. Just as clearly, it is vitally necessary to run your own financial life, for nobody will watch your personal financial business as carefully as you will watch it yourself.

What a sound financial adviser will do is to help you understand and evaluate the whole range of investment alternatives available for your IRA money—and the rest of your money, as well—within the context of your own plans and goals. The adviser will recommend, but it is up to you to make the necessary decisions, and you can decide well only if you have taken the time and trouble to become competent in investment matters.

For some, those fortunate to work where company-paid

financial planning is a fringe benefit, highly skilled financial planning advice is right at hand. If you do work for such a company, use that fringe as much as possible, for often you are getting the kind of financial planning help that only the wealthy can afford as individuals. Such professional personal financial planners may charge anywhere from $5,000 to $30,000 for developing full-scale plans for their wealthy clients, and yearly fees besides.

For small investors, the costs associated with such fee-based financial planning can create a problem. You can certainly buy some sort of computerized package plan that gives you very general—and usually not terribly useful—advice, but this is not the sort of very specific, personally relevant advice you want from a financial planner. On the other hand, you can get all the detailed recommendations you might possibly expect from any of the thousands of eager sellers of financial instruments you meet out there, and for nothing at all, if you are willing to settle for self-interested selling talk rather than sound financial planning and specific investment advice.

In fact, one way or another your financial planner will have to be compensated for the time spent working with you, and at least some of that compensation is likely to come from commissions generated by the planner's recommendations. Yes, that surely opens the door to self-interest and unethical dealing, and every financial planner knows that, as does every client who has thought the matter through. At the same time, it is the reality of the matter, a reality that is being handled successfully by ethical financial planners and astute clients every day of the week. The truth is that clients who innocently and trustingly—and ignorantly—place their financial affairs entirely in the hands of people they have just met, simply because they call themselves financial planners, will inevitably meet some who take them for all they have, some who honestly but ineptly accomplish much the same result, and many more who will help them in spite of themselves.

Ethical financial planners will help you to understand

your own needs and goals, and then move on from there to financial analysis and recommendations. You should be cautious about financial advisers new to you, skeptical about specific recommendations arrived at too easily and quickly, and extremely hesitant about a financial planner you sense is selling you anything at all. Yes, some of the recommendations of an ethical financial planner may also generate commissions, but that alone should not be a bar to going further with that planner. The main thing is to become fully satisfied that your financial planner is compatible with you, and has the kind of honesty, competence, and experience you want, along with the ability to help you execute the recommendations made.

There are tens of thousands of ethical, experienced financial planners in the country, and most are members of either the International Association of Financial Planners (5775 Peachtree-Dunwoody Road, Suite 120-C, Atlanta, Georgia, 30342, 404/252-9600), or the Institute of Certified Financial Planners (3443 South Galena, Suite 190, Denver, Colorado, 80231, 303/751-7600). You may also encounter professional financial planners who are employed by banks to provide assistance to customers, sometimes without fee. Some accounting firms, notably the larger ones, also supply financial planning services, generally at considerable fees; usually those services are performed by firm accountants. The overwhelming majority of these financial planners are entirely ethical practitioners, although you will, of course, encounter some who are not, as in every field.

Some planners work on a fee-only basis, while others will charge either a modest fee, perhaps $150 to $300, for initial consultations, with possible additional compensation from commissions generated by their recommendations. Others may charge no fee at all for initial consultations, relying upon commissions for their compensation. Some may make money on as little as a total $200 fee, when all that is being supplied is a generalized computer printout "financial plan," rather than fully developed personal advice. But skilled financial planners who charge from $150 to $300 for full-scale planning advice, which must by its nature involve at least two substantial planning sessions with you plus a good deal of study of your situation in between sessions, cannot possibly make any money on that fee. Then the fee is merely a screening device, aimed at making sure that you are very serious about developing a planning relationship. Whether that kind of planner charges you or not, the main compensation received will be in commissions, and probably in commissions derived from many years of working with you.

Fee or not, it makes sense to develop that kind of long-term relationship with a financial planner, for your developing IRA funds and for the entire set of lifetime financial plans that must be made, watched carefully, and revised as often as necessary. An investment program for your IRA money cannot possibly make any sense, unless it is part of a larger picture of lifetime financial plans.

You can seek a financial planner by directly writing to or calling one of the two main associations mentioned earlier, or for that matter by responding to a newspaper advertisement. But it is far better and more usual to seek one by direct recommendation from friends or associates who are satisfied clients of a financial planner and who are happy to recommend that planner to you. Planners are also very commonly recommended by such other professionals as accountants and lawyers, and sometimes also by insurance people, brokers, and bankers. The quality of the recommendation is crucial; that someone at a social gathering recommends a planner who is "making me a bucketful of money" should leave you entirely cold, while the reasoned recommendation of your accountant, lawyer, or a close friend may cause you to call for an appointment. No seasoned, ethical financial planner touts any kind of investment, or even recommends anything at all, on first interview. Quite the opposite; the real professional takes pains to tell you that you will not get rich quick, is likely to recommend rather conservatively, and may also strongly suggest that you make such terribly unpalatable changes as spending less on consumables.

However good the recommendation, though, there are many questions to ask and factors to consider when talking with a possible financial adviser for the first time. Here are the main matters to examine, taken from *The Manager's Lifelong Money Book*, my most recent book on full-scale personal financial planning.

■ If anyone is giving you a recommendation, you will want to know how long and how well the recommender has known the planner, and to try to learn everything you can about the planner before your first meeting.

■ If you are getting a recommendation from another professional, such as an accountant, lawyer, banker, broker, or insurance representative, will that person get any sort of payment for the referral? There is nothing particularly wrong about that sort of referral fee, but it is certainly something you want to know about going in, and from whoever is doing the recommending, rather than from the planner, who should not have to reveal this if someone else has not been willing to do so. Many professionals will freely tell you about a referral fee without even being asked, but if you ask and the response to your question is evasive, you may have a problem, with recommender or planner or both.

■ When you call the planner to make an appointment, ask that any available printed material be sent to you first; allow enough time to receive and read the material before the meeting.

■ At that first meeting, you should ask about the planner's experience, both as a full-scale financial planner and in any other finance-related matters. In this kind of consulting relationship, relevant experience counts a very great deal, and unseasoned neophytes are only that, no matter how well formally educated.

■ At the same time, you also want to know about the education of the planner; professional association certifications and college financial planning degrees and courses can be very helpful, if some basic experience is there.

■ What kinds of clients does the planner have, in terms of their occupations, income levels, and resources? If quite a few of them are like you, then you may be talking with someone who will easily and helpfully respond to your goals and needs. If not, you may be dealing with someone who is a bad fit, no matter how skilled and personally congenial.

■ What specific referrals to satisfied existing clients will the planner supply? If none, walk away, with all deliberate speed. If some, be very sure to call them to discuss as much as they are willing to discuss, asking them the same kinds of searching questions you would ask anyone recommending the planner. This kind of careful call is highly desirable, no matter how strong any initial recommendation.

■ Will someone else in the office actually be handling your planning? If so, then your basic queries must include that person, even if that requires a full second interview.

■ How will the day-to-day, week-to-week relationship actually work? Whom will you call when you have a question or comment, or want to make a move? Will the planner be calling you to suggest moves, as laws and investment situations change?

■ What will your financial plan look like? This is the planner's cue to offer to show you some reasonably appropriate plans developed for other people in your general circumstances, of course without revealing their identities.

■ How often will you and the planner update your plan? The answer should be at least once a year, with you supplying everything the planner needs to do the job well.

■ What will it all cost? This should be a very complete discussion of initial fees, commissions for the several kinds of financial planning moves you might make through the planner, and recurring costs, as for a yearly plan review. Do not take for granted that all transactions will flow through the planner's office, though many will. For example, you may very well want to use a discount broker for some kinds of transactions.

■ After the initial meeting, discuss what you have learned with others, including your professional advisers and whomever else you think might be helpful.

■ Should you decide to go ahead to make a financial plan, also carefully discuss the finished plan with the key people in your financial life. In financial planning, some of the earliest recommendations a planner makes may involve some of the most important financial moves you will ever make. These early recommendations often require financial restructuring in such vitally important areas as life and health insurance, major investments, and retirement planning. They are coming from someone you cannot yet know very well, no matter how carefully you have investigated and directly queried the planner, and should be treated very carefully indeed. Remember that while inaction is itself often a very costly error, ill-considered action is at least as great a threat.

Once you have your general financial house in order, you can focus on building the kind of long-term "security blanket" your IRA can be.

3

A Review of IRA Basics

You can reasonably expect the basic rules governing IRAs to change many times during your lifetime. Some have changed as a result of the 1986 tax law; others will change as the years go by. In aggregate, these are major funds that are accumulating; by early 1986, total IRA funds had topped $200 billion, and were growing at an accelerating rate, as both savings and yield continued to build up. Funds like that—held by millions of small savers and investors who have little special-interest political power—draw revenue-hungry politicians like chickens draw hawks. There will therefore be continuing pressure to tax IRAs and IRA-related transactions as these funds grow.

On the other hand, there will also be pressure to raise contribution limits as a means of softening the impact of budget cuts as attacks on Social Security continue. And there will be special-interest pressures of other kinds, as well, not least from those investment community people whose products are disadvantaged or prohibited as IRA investments. What you can be sure of, though, is that there will be rule changes. It is and will remain necessary to carefully keep up with IRA rules over the years, for changes will affect both how you handle your IRAs and what investments you can and should make with IRA money.

The Basic Tax Advantage in IRAs

Although the 1986 tax law has made some changes in current IRA rules, what is by far their most important tax advantage has been left as is. Actually, that most basic advantage has been enhanced, and largely because of the new situation created by the law itself. At a time when capital gains taxes have gone up very sharply, and when many previously available tax shelters have disappeared, *your IRA funds will continue to accumulate tax free.*

That is an enormous advantage, and especially so for anyone intending to use even a small part of their long-term financial planning funds to buy and sell stocks, bonds, and other securities. For that reason alone, whether or not your yearly contributions are tax deductible, it will pay you handsomely in the long run to set up an IRA. Put whatever you can into it up to the legal limits, and create what can become a tremendously valuable tax-free trading fund with the money—not a speculative fund, a trading fund. You may not necessarily invest now; your current situation may call for using your IRA money differently. But sooner or later—and probably sooner—that IRA fund, accumulating without capital gains taxes, will emerge as one of your primary long-term means of building a very meaningful later-years stake. Capital gains taxes under the new tax law can go as high as 35%, and even more, once you take all federal, state, and local capital gains taxes into account. Later on in your life, capital gains taxes may rise still higher. The difference between a tax free investment fund and one subject to these capital gains taxes can be one of the most important personal financial facts of your lifetime.

Right after passage of any major tax law—and the 1986 law was a big one—it is natural to focus on the changes. But the fact is that for the vast majority of Americans the new tax law left IRA rules substantially unchanged.

If you are not covered by any other pension plan, you can take full advantage of your IRA contribution tax deductions, as before. You can put up to $2,000 of earned income each year into a tax-sheltered IRA fund, taking every dollar put in as a tax deduction. If you and your nonworking spouse (you must be legally married) set up funds, the total earned income put in can be $2,250, rather than the $2,000 you could put in alone. You and your working spouse can each put in up to $2,000 of earned income every year, for a total of $4,000 per year, and all that money will be deducted from your tax returns for that year. Any money put in up to April 16 of the following year can be a deduction for the previous tax year. Your IRA contributions must be in cash, and cannot be in property.

The rest of the contribution rules are rather uncomplicated. Everything you put into an IRA has to be out of directly earned income; for example, you can't put in $2,000 or $2,250 when you have earned only $1,500 that year, but must limit your contribution to only that $1,500. Earned income does not include such unearned income sources as pensions, dividends, and interest. You can start an IRA with as small an amount as your bank, securities firm, or other IRA trustees will accept, sometimes as little as $50, contribute to it as often as you wish or the trustees will accept, and contribute in any year as little as nothing or as much as the legal limits. You can also have as many IRAs as you wish, for as many purposes as there are different kinds of IRAs but your total contribution cannot be more than the legal limit in any year.

Note that by "covered," the law means eligible for pension plan coverage. If you are employed and there is some sort of pension plan available, you are defined as covered and there are then some possible restrictions on your ability to take tax deductions for your IRA fund contributions. But only on the deductions—there are no taxes on the buildup of your IRA fund once your money is in it.

Note also that there is a minor change in the new tax law: you can now set up a "spousal" IRA even if the spouse classified as nonworking is actually making a couple of hundred dollars in any year.

Even most people employed and with pension plans available as a result of that employment have no substantial IRA rule changes. A married couple with an adjusted gross income of up to $40,000 can fully deduct all IRA contributions from their tax return. So can a single person with an adjusted gross income of up to $25,000. Note that this is adjusted gross income, not full gross income, which is a good deal higher.

The deductibility gets phased out over the next $10,000 of adjusted gross income figures and the amount phased out is proportionate to the amount put into the IRA in a given year. For example, if a married couple puts in $2,000, in a year when adjusted gross income is $40,000, the whole $2,000 is deductible. If the adjusted gross income had instead been $45,000 that year, only half, or $1,000, would have been deductible. If the adjusted gross income had been $50,000 or more that year, nothing would have been deductible. For single taxpayers the deduction phases out the same way, between $25,000 and $35,000 of adjusted gross income. For married people filing separately with $40,000 to $50,000 of combined income, the deduction phases out against that portion of combined income that is over $40,000, and against the contribution of the lower earner.

The 1986 tax law also provides that nondeductible IRA contributions will not be taxed on their distribution back to you later on, although the money you make on those contributions while in your IRA will be taxable. For example, if you have put $20,000 of nondeductible money into your total IRA funds over a period of years and those total IRA funds have grown to $200,000 later in life, 10% of every dollar you then get back out will be nontaxable. All the rest will be taxable, for it will include both originally deductible contributions and money you have made on all your IRA funds. But do note that the way the law sets out for accomplishing this taxation is quite likely to prove wholly unworkable, and by the time you start getting money out of your IRA much may have changed in this area. This is the sort of thing that plagues tax professionals, but has little to do with either basic IRA advantages or your own saving and investing choices.

Withdrawals and Penalties

The IRA was conceived by many of its Congressional framers as a very long-term kind of fund, functioning as an optional addition to Social Security and any other pension funds. They therefore made it difficult to withdraw IRA money without penalty. Funds can be withdrawn, if desired, starting at the age of 59½, but if money is taken out earlier (except in circumstances of complete disability or terminal illness), a 10% penalty tax on the amounts withdrawn must be paid, on top of ordinary income taxes on those sums.

Clearly, it is desirable to avoid the penalty tax, and to try very hard to find other sources of needed money that cost less than tapping your IRA. The IRA creates so superb a set of investment opportunities that it is most advantageous to put the maximum allowable in every year and watch it grow rather than to withdraw any of it, unless you absolutely must. But you should not let any concern about possible future withdrawal needs and consequent 10% penalties stop you from making the largest possible IRA contributions every year. *Even if you must withdraw money and pay a 10% penalty tax on it, you will still be much further ahead than had you paid taxes and invested the after-tax remainder.*

Consider, for example, a five-year-old IRA fund worth $27,000, which otherwise would have been an ordinary after-tax investment fund of only $14,000 after five years. You could withdraw $13,000 from your IRA, pay ordinary income taxes and 10% penalty taxes on the withdrawn money, and yet be far ahead, for then you would have realized $5,000 to $10,000 in cash, depending upon your tax bracket, and you would *still* have a $14,000 IRA. Further out, the IRA's advantages become even more apparent; ten years out the IRA fund is over twice the size of the fully taxed fund. Twenty years out it is worth two and a half times as much, as the compounding of yield held in the fund builds growth on growth. At that time, you could expect to be able to take as much as $100,000 out of your IRA funds, pay income taxes on it, pay a penalty tax of $10,000 on top of that, and still have a $100,000 fund left, which is as much as you would have had in all had you never started and built the IRA fund.

So do not worry about penalty taxes on premature withdrawals of IRA money, unless you know that you will need the money out within just a few years of putting it in. Exactly when the penalty tax on that kind of premature withdrawal is cancelled out by the growth in the fund cannot be predicted, because it depends on your IRA's yield and your top tax bracket in all the years involved, but it would be about five years out, assuming that you take all the money out of your IRA fund. But if you have to take out only a few thousand dollars, especially in a year when your income is relatively low, your IRA-generated extra gains may cancel out the 10% tax penalty as early as the third year.

In the normal course of events, you can without penalty begin to withdraw money from your accumulated IRA funds at age 59½, though you can, if you wish, keep your IRA funds intact and accumulating until you are 70½. At 70½, you *must* begin to withdraw your money, to avoid really damaging tax penalties. The amounts you must withdraw will depend on the actuarial tables in effect at that time, which may be very different from those being used today. For example, if your life expectancy at 70½ is then 20 years, and your IRA funds total $1,000,000, you will have to take out 5% of your fund, or $50,000, in that first year.

You can, at any time after 59½, take out as much as you wish without the 10% penalty tax, but withdrawals will be subject to ordinary income tax, and you are therefore likely to withdraw only as much as you need. The next year, the minimum withdrawal will be one-nineteenth of your IRA fund, which will by then have increased again, and probably far more than your minimum withdrawal of the previous year. And so on; in this example, you will have withdrawn all your IRA funds by age 95½.

The tax penalty for failure to withdraw the legal minimum in any year is severe—50% of what should have been withdrawn but was not. That would mean a punitive tax of $25,000, if you withdrew only $25,000 rather than the $50,000 minimum. This is a very large penalty indeed; those who reach 70½ will have to be very careful to withdraw at least the legal minimums from their IRAs every year.

The IRA Rollover Account

The law provides a very significant IRA tax shelter opportunity for lump-sum funds resulting from termination of several other kinds of pension plans. Many such lump-sum distributions would otherwise be a tax disaster, for then the money involved would be taxed as income, averaged over 5 years, and therefore at very high rates. But since the coming of IRAs, that kind of disaster need not happen in the overwhelming majority of such situations, for you have 60 days to set up an IRA rollover account for each such terminating plan. The money so "rolled over" will from then on be accorded the same very favorable tax-advantaged treatment that all your IRA money is given.

You can, for example, roll over all the money in your corporate pension plan on retirement from a company. You can also roll over such funds when a company leaves you, as when it goes out of business or terminates existing plans.

It is possible, then, and perhaps probable, that many will

find themselves holding several such IRA rollover accounts in their lifetimes, all running simultaneously, for such accounts cannot be consolidated with each other or with other IRA accounts that are regularly added to. Many of these rollover accounts are very large IRAs, some of them starting with hundreds of thousands of dollars' worth of previously accumulated pension funds. A pension fund that has been building for the past 25 years and is then rolled over into an IRA is for all practical and real-dollar purposes just like the million-dollar IRAs previously discussed.

Note that with these large funds some questions can arise that do not yet affect plans that have been accumulating at the rate of a few thousand dollars a year for several years. For example, with large rollover IRA funds invested for maximum safety in federally insured bank obligations, *you must be very careful to keep each IRA account under the $100,000 federal insurance limit*, and to figure in the interest and compounding of that interest in the coming year as you adjust your IRA account holdings. You can have as many IRA accounts as you wish, without limitation, and several accounts, if necessary, for a single rollover fund.

Note also that the term *rollover* has other meanings, as well, which have nothing to do with the IRA rollover account. Several kinds of continuations of financial arrangements are commonly called rollovers in the world of business and finance, as when a bank continues a line of credit, or when you continue to loan money to a bank by taking out a new CD when your old one expires.

There are two other IRA-related kinds of rollovers:

1. You are said to be rolling over your IRA money when you take out all or part of an account in cash, which you may do once a year without tax penalty, *as long as you put the money back into an IRA account within 60 days of withdrawal*. Any IRA funds kept over 60 days are treated as penalty withdrawals— that is, as ordinary income in year withdrawn and also subject to 10% penalty taxes.

Some IRA account holders have treated the 60-day withdrawal period without penalty as a kind of short-term source of funds, and it can be used that way. But that is chancy; if you need cash badly enough to have to use your IRA funds that way, the odds are that you will have difficulty in putting the money back during the 60-day period, and will wind up with a very substantial penalty. It is far safer to try hard to borrow needed money than to treat IRA funds in this way.

2. You are said to be rolling over your IRA money when you move it from account to account, rather than as cash into your own hands. That can be done in an unlimited way, with as much money and as often as you like and through as many accounts as you have or care to set up. It is accomplished by a letter of instruction to the trustee of the account from which money is being moved. In this way, you can set up new accounts and move money between such trustees as banks, brokerage accounts, and mutual funds. There will usually be a small transaction charge levied by the trustee letting go of some of your money, in the $5 to $20 range, but that is understandable, as there are handling costs involved. There may also sometimes be delays in processing your written instructions. This is also understandable, for some trustees have shown themselves to be reluctant to part with very profitable IRA money in their possession—but it is not acceptable.

The Question of Bankruptcy

For lifetime personal financial planning, it is very important to note that your accumulating IRA funds are probably safe from ordinary creditors, should you at any time be forced to declare personal bankruptcy. "Probably" is better than "surely" here, for the issue has not yet been fully and absolutely conclusively settled in the courts, and the protection can also be changed by law in the future.

However, it should also be noted that this protection is far from absolute, as it does not include protection against

Internal Revenue Service claims, which can reach through the shield of personal bankruptcy. Nor does it shield against specific exceptions, as when Congress allows student loan administrators to reach through personal bankruptcy to try to collect on unpaid loans.

Investment Restrictions

IRA funds may be invested in a wide range of possible vehicles, and much of the rest of this book is devoted to a discussion of those vehicles as they fit into an IRA investment strategy. First, though, it should be pointed out that IRAs are by law prohibited from being used in several kinds of investments and investment moves.

Those investment restrictions were built into the law by Congress as a means of attempting to direct IRA holders into relatively safe, rather than highly speculative, investments and investment techniques. IRAs were and are seen by Congress as long-term portable personal pension plans, rather than as vehicles for speculation. An IRA holder can still speculate, for example, in volatile stocks, but not with borrowed money in a margin account.

Here are the main areas of restriction:

1. You cannot buy gold, silver, or gemstones with IRA money, except for new gold and silver coins issued by the Federal government. Lawmakers saw these as nonproductive speculations (although some may very well disagree), rather than investments, and they are directly prohibited by law. However, nothing in the law precludes purchase of shares in companies involved in mining or trading gold, silver, and gemstones, for these are clearly investments, and no different in kind from any other stock purchases.

2. You cannot use IRA money to buy life insurance, when the purchase is primarily a life insurance policy, even though that policy may have some savings and investment features. You cannot therefore buy term insurance, which is purely life

insurance. Neither can you buy straight (also known as whole life) insurance—that is, life insurance with cash surrender values building up inside the policy at the same time the policy insures your life. Nor can you buy the newer universal or variable life insurance policies, which are essentially whole life policies that build up cash surrender values somewhat faster, while insuring your life.

You can, however, buy an annuity, which ultimately pays you during your lifetime, or your survivors should you die before the full operation of the annuity. That is really a life insurance policy, too, but is seen by lawmakers as primarily an investment instrument with life insurance features, rather than as primarily a life insurance policy.

Yes, certainly, these are rather fine distinctions, and will very probably alter over the years, as insurance industry lobbyists have a continuing and powerful impact upon lawmakers. But this is the way the restriction on life insurance purchase works as of this writing.

3. You cannot use IRA money to buy collectibles other than the previously mentioned gold and silver coins. That has been the law since 1982, and some IRA accountholders bought collectibles for their IRAs before then. Those holding collectibles in their IRAs can continue to do so, storing those collectibles with the trustees of their IRA accounts. But if they sell those collectibles they cannot replace them with other collectibles, and must otherwise invest the sales proceeds.

4. You cannot use borrowed money in transactions for your IRA account. That is a very important restriction, for it eliminates several kinds of investment instruments and techniques, all of which depend on leverage—that is, the use of borrowed money to try to make money. Therefore, you cannot operate an IRA stock trading account—a self-directed account (of which more in later chapters)—on a margin basis, with your broker lending you part of the money you use for stock purchases.

Similarly, you cannot use IRA money in real estate

purchases that include such borrowings as mortgages and builders' loans. Therefore, you cannot use your IRA to buy into the vast majority of real estate investments. Those real estate investments that include no such borrowings are legal for IRAs.

For the same reasons, you cannot buy futures with IRA money, for the borrowing element is central to the transaction.

5. You cannot use IRA money to sell stock short—that is, to sell borrowed stock at a profit if that stock goes down—for that is seen as very much like using borrowed money in IRA transactions.

6. You cannot use IRA funds as security for a loan.

The Kinds of IRA Accounts

Sometimes there seem to be a thousand sellers out there, each with a significantly different kind of IRA account to sell, each promising more safety, a higher rate of return, and better service than anyone else. In the IRA selling game, there is a great deal of play with misleading offers, seductive numbers, and fine print. But the truth is that there are really just a few basic kinds of arrangements. There are also some charges to watch out for, and of course there are your own investment goals to keep in mind at all times.

The truth is also that no matter how hard sellers try to push a one-stop-shopping concept for IRAs—and other financial services, as well—there is as yet no such thing in existence. As your IRA funds grow, you will find yourself needing to do business with several kinds of IRA providers in order to develop your IRA money into the balanced, major, lifelong personal pension plan it can and should be. On the other hand, some organizations do provide two or more different kinds of IRA accounts, often by arrangement and commission-sharing with other kinds of IRA providers. That can sometimes mean modest transactions savings for you, though it can mean some confusion and possible entrapment as well.

For example, a bank may offer an IRA built around rather standard certificates of deposit. In most instances, those certificates of deposit will be federally guaranteed, up to specified amounts, and the IRA account will be sold hard and accurately by the bank as safe because of the federal deposit insurance guarantee. The same bank, however, may very well have acquired or have selling arrangements with a stock brokerage firm, which is offering wholly different kinds of self-directed IRA stock trading accounts that are in no way insured by the federal government. The bank does not fraudulently claim that these kinds of accounts are federally insured, and may even go out of its way to tell you that they are not. But the fact that they are offered through a bank may make them somehow seem safer to many people than IRA stock trading accounts offered by nonbanking financial organizations.

The truth, of course, is that the bank-offered trading account is neither more nor less safe than any equivalent account. As so many hundreds of thousands of us have found out to our dismay in recent years, banks are no safer places to keep money than anywhere else; what creates safety is the federal deposit insurance guarantee, and without that many banks are very risky indeed.

In a certain sense, there are really only two basic kinds of IRA arrangements, the same two basic arrangements that exist throughout the world of personal investment. On the one hand, you can put your money into the hands of financial professionals, who for a price—and there is always a price, one way or another—invest your money for you, usually (but not always) subject to your periodic evaluation of their success in so doing. That is what you do when you open a bank-administered IRA, whether the bank involved is a commercial bank, a savings bank, a savings and loan association, or a credit union. That is also what you do when you open an IRA administered by a mutual fund or an insurance company or one run by your employer or professionals hired by your employer. On the other hand, you can open a self-directed IRA, in which you make many of the same kinds of investing decisions that are made for you when you put your money into the hands of professionals.

In another, more routine sense, there are five basic kinds of IRAs. At present, these include bank-administered IRAs of several kinds; the IRAs offered by the many kinds of mutual fund organizations; insurance company IRAs featuring annuities; company-sponsored IRAs; and self-directed stock brokerage account IRAs, capable of being invested in a whole range of securities. Each of these kinds of IRAs and their costs, will be discussed, many more than once, in the chapters that follow.

4

Certificates of Deposit for IRAs

By far the most common kind of IRA is one administered by banks and funded by bank-issued certificates of deposit (CDs). Commercial banks, savings banks, savings and loan associations, and credit unions all actively promote such IRAs, in the process generating a wide variety of selling offers with seeming differences among them.

These banking institutions also may offer other kinds of IRAs, as when a stock brokerage subsidiary of a bank attaches the bank's name to a mutual-fund-based IRA or a self-directed brokerage account IRA. These are not to be confused with CDs; but it is increasingly easy to do so, as a horde of eager sellers continue to try to make their offerings seem both safer and more lucrative than the rest. In these circumstances, it becomes very important to completely understand what a CD is and is not, what the investment implications of the several kinds of CDs really are, and what protections are and are not present when you buy a CD from a banking institution.

A "certificate" of deposit is really any valid evidence that you have an interest-bearing deposit in a banking institution.

The investment is that deposit itself, and that deposit is a loan by you to the banking institution, with interest and repayment terms specified by the bank's offer, which you have accepted by making your deposit/loan to the bank. In this widest sense, any bank deposit can be used to fund your IRA, including the time deposits generally known as CDs, the demand deposits known as passbook savings accounts, and everything in between, including short- and long-term deposit/loan arrangements with both fixed and variable rates of interest.

That is, in fact, how the modern consumer-targeted CD has developed; you can now get a CD for almost any amount or term you want, with interest fixed or variable. And that can become a little confusing, especially since consumer CDs first developed as rather standard packages: six-month to seven-year bank obligations, with fixed interest rates and large minimum purchases mandated by law. But the laws have been changed; we are now in the middle of the new financial marketplace, and both CDs and IRAs are matters of hot competition among several kinds of sellers.

That CDs are by far the most popular kinds of IRA investments is entirely understandable, in terms of both the history and current safety of the instruments. From the first, IRAs have been regarded, by Congress and by most investors, as long-term personal savings plans, best suited for the least risky funding possible, even if that meant building them somewhat slowly. Financial professionals quite correctly see most IRA accountholders as essentially "risk-averse," although some have been willing to take risks and more are doing so as IRA holdings grow.

It is also a matter of historical coincidence that IRAs have become possible and popular while bank interest rates have been very high relative to inflation. Indeed, the early 1980s were times of great opportunity for the risk-averse, as the pace of inflation lagged far behind available, safe rates of interest. For the first time in several decades, it became possible to safely make 4% to 8% more in real dollars than the pace of inflation, and in those circumstances IRAs funded by CDs became extremely and quite rightly attractive to the great majority of new IRA accountholders.

Most bank CDs have been very safe in this period, for most have been fully federally guaranteed, up to $100,000 per IRA account. That has meant a great deal to the risk-averse, as Congress has intended ever since the 1930s, when federal insurance of bank deposits went into effect. And it has been particularly so in the volatile, highly speculative financial markets of the 1980s. Large numbers of Americans quite correctly see the new financial marketplace as an extremely risky, fraud-filled jungle, and want to do their necessary journeying in that jungle as safely as possible.

The Significance of Federal Insurance

That federal insurance of your deposit is crucial. Without it, a bank CD is merely a bank's promise to pay you, at a time when banks have failed and continue to fail all over the country. In this period even the promise of the largest banks in the country, some of them the largest in the world, is just not good enough. The near-failure of the Continental Illinois Bank proved that conclusively, for only the intervention of the federal government saved that huge bank and its depositors from a devastating failure that might have brought down much more.

There is absolutely no guarantee that any bank, no matter how large, will be saved by government, for federal administrations, attitudes, and needs can change while your money is sitting there in a bank's CD. The only meaningful guarantee is the federal guarantee of each individual account, and even that can change in years to come. Not now, but maybe later. It is prudent to watch conditions closely, even when your money is in a federally guaranteed bank account.

Let me make the point even more strongly, for this matter of watching your money, taking no guarantees for granted, and therefore not tying up your money so that you cannot get at it should basic conditions change, is quite central to everything else in this book. In five previous financial planning books, I have warned of personal disasters in bank accounts that were not federally insured. In each instance, the predicted disasters came between the time of writing and the time of publication—faster, worse, and in ways no one had foreseen.

It is unlikely that the federal government will absolutely refuse to make good on its bank account guarantees at any time in the near future, but there can come a time, for example, when a hard-pressed federal government may drag its feet on mass bank insurance payments, while failing to check a roaring inflation, the net effect being to pauperize those caught with their funds in failed banks. No matter how they look on the surface, these are extraordinarily difficult, dangerous times. You must be sure to set things up so that you can get at your funds if you feel you must, and watch carefully to see if the time has come to do so.

Then why an IRA, with its penalties for early withdrawals? Why not keep everything liquid and short-term, even if full taxes must be paid and yields kept low? Because the failure or reluctance of the federal government to keep its solemn deposit insurance promises is a "worst case," which can—but probably will not—happen. And because tax-advantaged IRAs grow so much faster than comparable taxable investments, it is possible to come out ahead even if you must invade the IRA only a few years after beginning to build it. The need in these years is to watch carefully and limit risk, not to panic.

In addition to making sure that your IRA (and other) bank deposits are federally insured, make sure that you have evidence in the form of a written confirmation that a deposit was really set up. That is standard bank procedure; the absence of such a procedure is unacceptable, and you should demand such a confirmation. At least once, it has happened that a bank sold instruments people thought were CDs, did not enter the instruments on its books, and then failed. The federal insurers then questioned the government's liability in that situation, arguing that money taken but not actually appearing on the bank's books as insurable accounts might not be covered. At this writing, the issue has not been resolved— and the bank's depositors have not been paid their government insurance.

If you are opting for the safety of a federally insured bank deposit, also make sure that what you are buying is precisely that. These days, your friendly neighborhood banker is quite likely also to be selling every financial instrument in sight, personally or through someone at a desk just across the way on the banking floor. If what you want is federal insurance, don't let yourself be talked into some wonderful tax-exempt bonds insured by a consortium of "absolutely reliable" private insurers. They are not as reliable as the federal government, and the bonds (more about them later) are likely to be wholly inappropriate for your IRA, besides.

These are the federal insurance organizations:

- The Federal Deposit Insurance Corporation (FDIC) insures deposits in savings and commercial banks.

- The Federal Savings and Loan Insurance Corporation (FSLIC) insures deposits in savings and loan associations.

- The National Credit Union Association (NCUA) insures deposits in credit unions.

Those are the organizations you are looking for, and they are usually stated as initials in the bank advertisements—FDIC, FSLIC, and NCUA. All three of them go up to $100,000 per account, and you can open as many IRA accounts as you wish in as many banks as you wish, one to a bank.

If a bank CD or other deposit account funding your IRA is not insured by one of the above, it is not nearly as safe an investment. Then it is like any other organization's promise to pay: only as good as the assets and business prospects of its maker. But here there are no rating organizations to help you evaluate the worth of that promise to pay, as there are with bonds, which are also organizational promises to pay. An IBM bond's promise to pay and a troubled Johns Manville bond's promise to pay are two entirely different things; this is easy to see and also easy to ascertain, for it is a matter of standard bond ratings. But that one bank's promise to pay is better or worse than another's is—for all but professionals who follow those banks—very difficult to determine.

That even puts it perhaps too gently, for these are hard times for banks, large and small. Banks that seem to turn large profits can in actuality be carrying hundreds of billions of dollars in bad foreign loans that will never be repaid—and a lot more in questionable domestic loans—and relying upon government to continue to misstate the real nature of the situation and to bail the banks out if other governments openly refuse to pay their debts. The truth is that for individuals holding CDs, in IRAs or out of them, the federal guarantee is everything.

The Enticements to Watch For

For banking institutions, IRAs are enormously profitable. There is a great difference between what the bank pays you in interest and what it makes in interest on your money when it loans it out again. That is why bank IRA charges, for both setup and continuance, are low to nonexistent. That is also why banks can afford promotional giveaways, interest come-ons, and very large advertising budgets when competing for your IRA money. Federal deposit insurance has given banks an enormous edge over all other IRA providers, as large numbers of risk-averse people will take low yields for the safety of the federal deposit guarantee.

As of this writing, bank CD rates, which were high in the

early 1980s, have dropped considerably, into the 5% to 7% area for six-month fixed-rate CDs, up to the 8% to 10% area for five- to seven-year CDs with a fixed rate, and in the lower part of that range for variable rates. The numbers themselves are of no concern, as they will have changed by the time you read this work. Their usefulness is that they illustrate the kind of difference between short- and long-term yields that has held for much of the last decade. They also point up the interest yield differences between CDs and the other major kinds of debt obligations we will examine later. A whole range of debt obligations pay more, as presumed safety dictates; only short-term Treasury obligations and some tax-advantaged municipals consistently pay less. More on this range of obligations in the chapters on debt obligations.

You do have to pay a good deal of attention to CD offers, for many of them are extraordinarily and quite purposefully misleading. In this area, we are a long way from the honest, conservative banker who could be relied upon to tell you the truth on financial matters. When bankers sell CDs, and especially when they are selling CDs as funding devices for extremely profitable IRA business, you can expect them to be as misleading as the slipperiest used car seller you will ever meet.

For example, you will run into the ad that advertises a wonderful 12.2% for a CD, when all other banks are offering 8% to 9%. A comeon, of course. That 12.2% is likely to be for just a month, maybe even a week, followed by the area's standard interest rates, and perhaps compounded infrequently, cutting actual interest yields. You are likely to wind up making an extra 4% for one week, which is about $0.80 per $1,000 deposited per year. Or perhaps even nothing extra, if the compounding is adverse.

Similarly, a bank may offer a cash bonus or some merchandise giveaway for buying a CD. They do no great harm, unless they somehow mislead enough to affect what should be a very sober investing decision.

On the other hand, the bank that advertises a higher than

normal rate of return may be misleading you somewhat more seriously, for the rate may apply only to longer-term CDs than you want to own, and you may find yourself making a hasty, wrong decision that can haunt you for years. As so many people have discovered in other periods, the long-term CD that looks so good today may not be all that good tomorrow, when interest rates have gone way up; and every day that you hold what has become a low-interest CD is a day of further opportunities lost.

The Vital Question of Term

The longer-term CD opens up several substantial financial planning questions; indeed, it goes to the heart of how to handle your IRA, and for that matter many of your other savings and investments. Sellers of CDs will without exception urge you to "lock in high current rates of interest," so that they may have your money to reloan at a profit. But whether or not that is really the best thing to do rests upon your estimates—if you can make them—of both the future course of interest rates and the need to keep your money so you can move it quickly, without great penalties. For some of your money, not in IRAs, those estimates may lead you to move your money right out of the banking and securities markets into such hard goods as gold, gemstones, and collectibles. As of this writing, these are prohibited vehicles for IRA money, however. For IRAs the alternatives are more limited.

What seems to have been established beyond a shadow of a doubt in the last decade and half is that no one can predict the course of interest rates for the medium term, three to seven years—which is precisely the duration of the longer-term CDs. That is not simply a matter of incompetent economists failing to predict well. Far from it. The predictive apparatus today's economists can bring to bear is quite impressive, as far as it can go. The problem is that it cannot go far enough, especially in the area of medium-term prediction.

Medium-term, we cannot predict economic trends without also considering the politics of the time. And the fact is that no predictive apparatus has been developed that can consistently tell us how the political side will go. All the world's main industrial economies are at least partially managed and manipulated by their governments for political and military ends, as well as economic, and the several aspects of money policy are very much part of the government's manipulative arsenal. In those conditions, no one can predict interest rate trends very far out.

What further seems clear is that this is an extraordinarily volatile and difficult period, as we have previously discussed. Stocks and other investment vehicles rise and fall with great velocity, as the stock market rise and subsequent break of late 1985 and early 1986 showed so clearly. What can best be described as a set of hydraulic relationships seems to have developed between the stock market and interest rates. When interest rates go up—or even threaten to go up—professional money managers begin to move money out of stocks and in the direction of interest-bearing securities, depressing stock prices. When interest rates go down—or even threaten to go down—they buy stocks in huge quantities, taking the stock averages up again.

In today's markets, you want at the very least to be able to handle your IRA funds or arrange to have them handled as flexibly as those professionals do; and you simply cannot accomplish that with the longer-term CDs. The problem is that if you try to respond to market realities by selling CDs before maturity you will have to pay a huge interest-rate penalty. Perhaps even worse, the presence of the penalty may stop you from making the right move at the right time, and thereby cost you even more than the penalty itself would have, in the long run.

These are not small penalties. Even on a one-year CD, the penalty may be a full month's downward adjustment on the interest rate for withdrawal before maturity—that is, before the full year has passed. In those circumstances, withdrawal three months after purchase can result in cutting total interest by a full third, down to the level of a poor-paying passbook account, or even lower. The penalties are larger on longer CDs; early withdrawal six months into an eighteen-month CD can mean six-month interest penalties that destroy all your earned interest.

Nor are consumer CDs negotiable instruments, as the larger certificates of deposit issued by banks are. These are normally issued in denominations of $100,000 or more, are short term, and are part of the commercial paper market. Consumer CDs today can be withdrawn early, with penalties, and are not negotiable. Watch and make sure that you have that withdrawal privilege, by the way; some people seeking to pull money out of CDs in the mid-1970s found that the fine print allowed banks to hold on to their money.

To partially avoid the early withdrawal interest penalty, you can usually borrow money from the bank, using your CD as collateral. Many banks provide for such a borrowing, often for about 1% more than the CD is paying, so that the early withdrawal then bears a 1% interest penalty for the life of the borrowing. Be sure that at least that privilege exists, if you do go into longer-term CDs.

Alternatives to longer-term CDs are discussed elsewhere in this work, including several kinds of bonds and bond-using mutual funds.

In some periods of relatively high interest rates, shorter-term CDs can have a very real place in your IRA planning. Many banks will sell you CDs for three months or less, though the main shorter-term CDs run six months to two years. You can very conveniently use such an IRA as a starter, as so many have done in recent years, and then, as your fund money grows, move funds out into other kinds of IRAs. This essentially uses the short-term CD as a kind of IRA savings account. It is tax-advantaged, pays in high interest periods a reasonably high short-term rate of interest, and allows you to be as flexible as you want to be.

Whether you buy CDs short or longer term, be sure that

the bank is instructed to reinvest your CDs when they mature, rather than merely rolling the funds into a passbook savings account paying much smaller rates of interest. You should be watching your CD maturity dates, but we all slip sometimes, and a missed maturity date can result in a substantial interest loss if you have not provided for automatic reinvestment.

It is by far best to watch maturity dates carefully, though, as you may want to move that money elsewhere. If you wait until maturity date has gone by, you'll face an unnecessary interest penalty.

The Wise Consumer

Finally, on IRAs funded by CDs, note that it can pay to shop around. There is no particular advantage in tying your bank IRA to your other banking arrangements. Aside from the comeons and giveaways, there is very real willingness on the part of some banking institutions to pay more than others for IRA deposits, and also to provide such considerable advantages as lower penalties for early withdrawals. One bank may offer as much as a full percentage point, or even two points, more than others. Another may offer an eighteen-month variable rate CD with a one-month interest penalty for early withdrawal, while another may charge a six-month interest penalty for the same kind of withdrawal. One bank may offer an effective one-point loan if you want to make early withdrawals, while another may have no such loan provisions and heavy early withdrawal penalties.

There is no standard pattern, for these are highly competitive matters; different banks are willing to set different yields and rules for their own internal reasons. The IRA deposit market is very much a buyer's market, favoring you. Indeed, some banks may make rather imprudent high-interest and low-penalty offers in order to secure those highly profitable IRA deposits. By all means take them up on their imprudent offers, *as long as you are absolutely sure that your accounts are federally insured.* But do not under any circumstances make the mistake of taking a bank's good-looking IRA offer, only to find later that the account you opened was not federally insured. It cannot be put too strongly: *Banking institutions that are not federally insured are usually very poor risks. Do not put your money into them under any circumstances, no matter how high their promised interest rates and how favorable the other terms offered.*

Similarly, longer-term CDs have for some years been paying considerably more than either short-term CDs or money market mutual funds, with five- to seven-year rates often as much as three full points more than six-months rates. In the 1970s, when that began to happen, the disparity between long- and short-term rates was largely a reflection of widespread conviction that interest rates, then at very high levels, would continue to stay up, at least yielding banks a profit on reloaned long-term CD money. And that has been true—so far. But it may not be so indefinitely, and the banking institution that has aggressively and successfully sold large numbers of high-interest, long-term CDs may ultimately regret having done so. In low-interest times, such banks may very well fail, being unable to make enough to pay promised interest rates, and their depositors may find themselves relying on federal deposit insurance to get their money back. Go for the federal deposit insurance guarantee; with bank IRAs, nothing else will do.

5

Bonds for IRAs

Before discussing the several kinds of bonds and other debt obligations as possible IRA investments, it will be useful to talk about the nature of bonds somewhat more generally. In today's financial marketplace, there are so many different kinds of debt obligations being sold, and in so many different kinds of packages, that it is often hard for IRA owners to understand what is out there, much less to understand how the various offerings may or may not fit into IRAs.

When you put your money into an interest-bearing bank account, you are loaning money to a bank for a price. The bank relends your money, trying to do so at enough profit (over what it pays you in interest) to pay its own expenses and make money on your money. That is the essence of the transaction, whether your loan to the bank takes the form of a CD or a demand deposit, like a passbook account, from which you can take back your money at any time.

When you buy a bond or any of the bills, notes, certificates, and other money market instruments that all together constitute the body of debt obligations traded in the world's bond markets, you are undertaking the banking function yourself, by directly loaning money to the bond issuer or purchasing an already-issued debt, in the form of an existing bond or other debt obligation. The terms of repayment during the life of the bond and the amount to be repaid when the bond's life ends are contained in the bond itself, although many bonds will fluctuate in value during their lifetimes. More on value changes shortly.

When you buy shares in a mutual fund holding bonds and other debt obligations, you are once again using an intermediary to participate in debt instrument ownership on your behalf. The investment professionals managing that mutual fund are, for a fee, then trading in debt instruments on behalf of you and the other shareholders—with you watching, checking profitability, and periodically reevaluating your participation in the mutual fund, if you are handling your financial affairs properly.

However you are holding bonds, you are ultimately lending your money to the issuer of those bonds, and therefore need to be able to form several opinions on the way toward a buying decision. The first of these, in today's rather chaotic, very chancy financial marketplace, is how well you can expect the issuer (or the bond's insurers) to keep the bond's promise to pay interest and repay principal, as stated by the terms of the bond. That is what determines the "quality" of the bond.

Considerable help is available when it comes to evaluating bond quality. Moody's and Standard & Poor's, the major bond quality rating services, are as close as the nearest fairly substantial public library or stock brokerage office. Bond ratings are set at the time of original issue and then updated as issuers' circumstances change. Both services start with top AAA ratings and work their way down through AA and A ratings into the Bs and Cs. At the AAA level, risk is thought to be minimal, with somewhat more risk but relative safety in other A ratings. In the high Bs, considerable risk starts, with the low B and all the C ratings very dangerous indeed, even though they may pay what seem very attractive yields.

The "risk" referred to here is risk of default on interest and principal repayment promises. Some bonds that are tradable may be rather safe in terms of interest and repayment but be subject to severe price fluctuations, as interest rates change.

Bonds and other debt obligations that are federally guaranteed are routinely awarded AAA status by the bond rating services. They bear the federal government's direct promise to pay, as does federal bank deposit insurance, and those promises are as good as any you will get anywhere. If you are going to participate in the financial marketplace at all, rather than burying food, guns, and gold in your back yard, federal obligations are to be seen as safe.

Note, though, that *not every mutual fund claiming to be federally insured is wholly federally insured;* a high-interest Ginnie Mae fund may be largely invested in fully federally guaranteed Ginnie Maes, but may also be investing in quite risky repurchase agreements (repos) to get a little extra interest and competitive edge; it pays to read the prospectus very carefully.

Corporate and municipal bonds run the whole gamut of ratings, all the way from "blue chip" AAA-rated major corporate issues to the properly low-rated "junk bonds" used by corporate raiders in their campaigns for corporate control and to the sometimes even lower-rated obligations of municipalities close to official bankruptcy, many of which are already in effective bankruptcy.

More than other investments, bond yields reflect the bond market's estimate of the safety of the bonds offered, with the safest yielding the least at issue and the riskiest yielding the most. The yield offered generally takes taxes on interest into account; that is why the safest of the municipals yield so little in percentage points. Borrowers in bond markets are competing for loan money, and therefore have to pay competitive rates of interest, with bond ratings taken very much into account by bond buyers. What determines the price you or your mutual fund must pay for a bond is therefore a combination of the bond market's estimate of the relative safety of that bond, its yield after tax factors have been taken into consideration, and the general rate of interest in the economy—the going rate—at the time the bond is issued.

Bonds already issued and currently traded also reflect these factors, and the bond market will adjust their market value to take them into account. For example, a bond issued at 100, at issue paying 9%, will be worth more if the going rate of interest declines, for the bond's locked-in 9% will be worth more than bonds issued later that pay only 7%. Then the market value of the earlier bond will go up, until it reaches a level at which its current value, with an adjustment for future interest promises, is equivalent to current 10% market yields. The calculation involved is complicated; the net effect is that the market values of bonds go up when current going interest rates are lower than the rates they pay, and are then said to be *selling at a premium*. Conversely, bonds go down when interest rates go up, for then their values must adjust in the other direction. Then they are said to be *selling at a discount*.

Changes in perceived safety of bonds can also cause price changes. The bonds of a company in great trouble may go down, or even be virtually unsalable, if the rating services recognize that the trouble exists and sharply revise their safety ratings downward, as from the As to the Cs. The bonds of a municipal will sharply decline if interest payments are postponed. Rerating upward later may enhance the market value of such bonds.

As previously noted, IRA owners need not take tax factors into consideration when evaluating bond yields. That is why municipals, which depend so heavily upon tax advantage for their appeal, should have little or no appeal as IRA investments, whether directly purchased or in mutual funds. Safety and yield without tax considerations must both be very carefully taken into account, and bonds must therefore be watched just as carefully as any other investments.

You should not "tuck away" a bond (or anything else) in your IRA (or anywhere else) and leave it there, unexamined, figuring that all you have to do is collect the interest and hold the bonds until repayment of principal at maturity. On all but federally guaranteed bonds, that is the height of imprudence in terms of safety, for companies and municipalities may falter and go under while you are confidently holding on to a promise to pay that can no longer be kept.

That is all a bond is: a promise to pay. If it has specific collateral behind it, it is *collateralized*, meaning only that there may be something to liquidate in part payment of bondholders should its issuer go under. If backed by the "full faith and credit" of its issuer, it is in truth nothing more than a bare promise to pay, and only as good as its maker.

Even on federally guaranteed bonds, where the question of safety is scarcely raised in these years, it is wise to watch the risk factors. Politicians repudiate solemnly made promises, especially when they are promises made by other politicians. But beyond safety, you must also watch tradable federal bonds for fluctuations based on interest rates.

The market values of bonds issued in low interest periods will be seriously hurt in periods of high interest rates, and if high interest continues for long periods you can be locked into bonds paying less than you should be earning. That is the classic dilemma of such a bondholder, who either must sell at a loss to get money out (so it can be otherwise invested or used) or must hold, possibly taking a similar loss over a long period, while hoping that interest rates will cooperate and the bonds will go up.

Note also that it is highly unlikely that you will really be able to lock in very favorable rates of interest many years out after purchase of long-term bonds. Most corporate bonds have provisions making them *callable*—that is, capable of being retired, often to be replaced by lower-paying bonds, after some years or in some circumstances. Many municipals have similar provisions, though some do not. Long-term federal bonds generally are not callable, according to the terms of the issue, but you can be very sure that the federal government will in the long run prove rather creative in finding ways to soften the impact of any too-high-interest promises it has made.

Federal Government Bonds and Other Federal Debt Obligations

With a national debt approaching two trillion dollars as of this writing, the federal government is by far the largest single source of debt obligations in the world. Indeed, the constant addition to and refinancing of the national debt have created so huge a volume of federal obligations that, in some periods, it threatens to crowd out corporate and municipal obligations. Very much helped by eager sellers, it has also created an ever-increasing variety of wholly or partly federally guaranteed obligations, mutual funds, and federal and federally backed agency obligations of many kinds.

Federal debt obligations and guarantees are now available in several forms; the following discussion covers the kinds of obligations themselves and their possible direct purchase by IRA owners. (Their several mutual fund and asset-based securities forms are discussed in separate chapters.) You will be able to buy some of these federal debt obligations directly for your IRA through a self-directed brokerage account IRA. Others are issued in such large denominations that direct purchases for IRAs are impractical; they are really available only through IRAs administered by mutual funds, insurance companies, and banking institutions.

Treasury Bills

The shortest term and safest of the federal debt obligations are the Treasury bills, which are issued for periods of three, six, and twelve months. These pay fixed rates of interest for the period of issue. Treasury bills (popularly called T-bills) are discounted in advance, meaning that on direct purchase you—and all other purchasers—will pay less than the face value of the bill, and at maturity three, six, or twelve months later will be repaid the face value of the bill. The difference between what you paid and what you later received is the interest earned.

Direct purchase of these obligations by IRA owners is rather unlikely in any but the worst of times, when there is serious doubt about whether the federally protected depositors of a failed national banking system might have to wait and wait for the government to pay off their deposit insurance claims, suffering losses and perhaps great hardship while waiting. Such a time may come again; it is not now. Direct purchase of Treasury bills by small investors was a popular and right move in the 1970s, when bill interest rates were much highter than the legally restricted passbook savings interest rates of that period. But in the 1980s, with deregulation of bank interest rates, it became practical to go into federally insured bank accounts that often yielded at least slightly more than Treasury bills, and with effectively equal safety. On balance, both bank-administered IRAs funded by short-term CDs and money market mutual fund IRAs have been and still are better ways to go than direct purchase of Treasury bills.

On the other hand, such direct purchase of Treasury bills certainly does have a place in the strategy of an IRA owner managing a substantial self-directed account, and using the Treasury bills as a convenient way of storing cash from time to time, as do investment professionals handling far larger sums. When stock markets decline sharply, or a runaway inflation develops, or market conditions are chaotic and unpredictable, it may make good sense to move some of the funds in a self-directed IRA into safe, very short-term Treasury bills, and be ready to move funds out of them when conditions warrant.

Longer-Term Treasury Obligations

Longer-term Treasury obligations may be called either notes or bonds. Issues of one to ten years are called *notes;* longer-term issues, up to thirty years, are called *bonds*. As a practical matter, they are identical bonded debt instruments, except for the length of time the government is promising to pay at a stated rate of interest.

Such bonds are sold at face value, and carry interest coupons that are literally clipped at stated intervals, on which the stated interest is paid. They have not, as of this writing, been callable—that is, capable of being retired by the government and replaced by lower-interest bonds—but that could always change, at least on new bonds issued.

The federal promise to pay embodied in these bonds is as good as any such promise can be. They will, however, fluctuate with market and interest conditions, as previously described, and must be watched as carefully as you watch any other basically sound investment. They are prime candidates for conservatively managed self-directed IRAs when their yields are relatively high; the longer-term bonds in some periods pay rates of interest competitive with longer-term bank CDs, and a couple of points higher than such short-term instruments as Treasury bills, short-term CDs, and money market mutual funds.

Note that these longer-term Treasury issues are tradable, and that gives them a considerable advantage over the longer-term CDs, in which you have "locked in higher long-term rates," and in so doing have also locked yourself into the instrument itself. If you think that interest rates are about to increase sharply, and want to sell what will then be a low-paying CD to take advantage of higher rates available otherwise, you will probably have to pay a large interest penalty to do so. But if you want to sell a highly negotiable federal government bond on the bond market—that is, through a broker—you can do so whenever you wish, taking gains and losses immediately. These federal bonds are safe, fully negotiable, and immediately salable on a huge, ready-to-buy set of national and international bond markets.

The "bond markets" are not organized trading exchanges, like the New York and London stock markets. Rather, they are a set of informal and very effective arrangements among a considerable body of investment and banking institutions around the world. It is through this worldwide network of bond traders that public and private bond issuers bring their bonds and other debt obligations to market, either directly or through groups of investment bankers organized into underwriting syndicates that buy and then redistribute the debt issues, often as wholesalers to other brokers, sometimes as direct resellers to the public, and sometimes both.

This underwriting function has led to the development of some major new kinds of bond forms in this period, including both the zero-coupon bond and the asset-based security, and may lead to the development of other new bond forms in the next decade. More on these new forms soon.

Savings Bonds

The federal government from time to time aggressively markets savings bonds, and in this period has raised savings bond yields so that they are reasonably competitive with some short- and medium-term bank CD rates, set an interest floor under which savings bonds cannot go, and made it possible for savings bonds to rise with general interest rate levels.

However, federal savings bonds cannot be negotiated or used as loan collateral and must be held for at least five years to avoid interest penalties. Their only really substantial benefit is their tax advantage, which provides for payment of taxes on interest only when the bonds are cashed in, and also provides for exemption of interest income from state and local taxes. But these are not advantages for IRA owners considering their purchase, for IRAs are already tax advantaged in both respects, and better.

So buy savings bonds, if you will, with taxable investment and savings money, rather than with tax-advantaged IRA money—and probably for patriotic, rather than investment, reasons.

Federal Agency Bonds

Beyond Treasury obligations, well over a dozen federal agencies have been authorized by Congress to issue debt obligations, and many of them do so. In the process, they have together created a major addition to the traditional bond markets and whole new kinds of mutual funds.

Such agencies as the Government National Mortgage Association (Ginnie Mae) and the Federal National Mortgage Association (Fannie Mae) have, in accordance with national policy, established huge new secondary mortgage markets—in essence, buying mortgages from banks and other lenders—and have funded such mortgage purchases from public debt issues. Such agencies as the Small Business Administration (SBA) have made hundreds of millions of dollars' worth of loans, and funded those loans with the proceeds of public debt issues. Such agencies as the Tennessee Valley Authority (TVA) have made capital investments in publicly owned enterprises, funding them with public debt issues.

The needs perceived by Congress have been great, the grants of power to raise money by public offerings have been rather sweeping, and the agencies involved have together therefore generated an enormous amount of federally guaranteed debt.

The bonds so created are tradable, run as little as three months and as much as three decades, and are routinely granted AAA status by the bond-rating organizations because of the unconditional federal guarantee of payment, which is just as good as the federal deposit insurance guarantee that makes federally insured CDs so attractive.

Even with their AAA ratings, these bonds have generally paid half a point to a full point more than comparable-length Treasury issues, and continue to do so as of this writing. Like other tradable bonds, they will, of course, fluctuate with interest rates, going up in market value when interest rates decline and down in value when interest rates rise. However, with small to nonexistent risk and relatively high interest rates, they are very attractive investments for self-directed IRAs, and are also often accessible through mutual funds. (For another look at these securities see Chapter 6.)

Some of them, as a practical matter, have been accessible only through mutual funds, for they have been issued in such high denominations that most small investors and their IRAs have not been able to purchase them directly. A $25,000 Ginnie Mae bond certificate is scarcely a normal IRA purchase. On the other hand, many fully federally insured agency bonds are issued in smaller denominations, and are well worth considering for direct IRA purchase, which can be easily accomplished through a self-directed account. Note also that many of the federal agencies involved have been issuing these bonds in smaller denominations in recent years; by the time you read this page even Ginnie Maes may be available in denominations that make direct purchase practical and desirable.

That is a trend to note, for many of the bond mutual funds, zero-coupon bonds, and asset-backed securities created out of these and other federal obligations have introduced very substantial costs and risks that do not exist when the bonds are directly purchased. That is because the investment professionals involved in creating these instruments have, as investment bankers, brokers, and managers, figured out how to make enormous profits out of the very brisk trade that has developed in these kinds of funds and securities. But as long as so many of these obligations are issued in such large denominations, it may still pay to invest in them indirectly, rather than directly; more on these instruments, and on their costs, risks, and possibilities when they are specifically discussed.

Another trend well worth noting is the development of federally related private bond-issuing organizations, such as the Federal Land Banks and the Student National Marketing Association (Sallie Mae). These have long been thought of as if they were, indeed, federal agencies—in effect, carrying federal guarantees because they are doing the federal government's work pursuant to national policy. Their AAA bond ratings have long reflected the view that, if they became financially troubled, they would surely be bailed out by Congress, and they have long been described as "quasi-governmental" in nature.

Don't you believe all that for a minute. These are private corporations, and in today's climate their federal charters and affiliations entitle them to nothing at all. If Congress wants to bail them out of trouble, it can; but it is in no way forced to do so, and may not in the precise crisis circumstances in which such institutions may be in deep trouble. These obligations are quite sound now, and may be so for decades, but they are most emphatically not federally guaranteed. They must be evaluated as much on their merits as if they were municipal or corporate bonds, carrying no meaningful guarantees beyond the full faith and credit of their issuers—that is, their bare promise to pay—and any collateral supplied by their issuers.

The land banks, for example, are in this period carrying billions of dollars' worth of very bad farm debts, and will need help from Congress again and again to stay afloat. At this writing, their collateral is grossly overstated, and they are holding on to enormous quantities of what would be regarded by an ordinary lender as very bad loans. In contrast, the student loan organization, which also has billions of dollars' worth of bad loans out, is getting collection help from the Internal Revenue Service, and will probably emerge from a difficult period relatively sound. Each is a private organization; each is federally related, but not federally guaranteed; each must be evaluated on its own record and prospects.

We can reasonably expect other federal agencies to be turned private—that is, to be *privatized*—in the coming period, as government attempts to unload large debt burdens, present and future, on the private sector. When that happens, understand that the relative safety of the obligations involved has changed very greatly—usually for the worse. Should that happen to debt obligations you are holding in your IRA, you should reevaluate those obligations. Some should probably be sold off and some held, depending upon what has been privatized and what additional insurance arrangements, if any, have been made then.

Municipals

Sometimes, in a book like this, it is right to spend as much time and space on what should not be done as on what should be done. That is how it is with municipals and IRAs: a writer may be entirely against the use of municipals as IRA investments, but feel it desirable to discuss municipals quite carefully, because they are sold so very aggressively to IRA owners.

The term *municipals* is applied to the debt obligations of all government bodies in the United States at lower than federal level. These are also called *state and local obligations*, as they are issued by tens of thousands of state, county, municipal, and other local governments and their related agencies. The municipal bond market that results is a subsection of the informal worldwide bond market discussed earlier.

The main advantage offered by the purchase of municipals is tax avoidance and consequent high net after-tax yield. For individuals in the higher tax brackets, that can be a very great advantage indeed, and wealthy individuals have been buying municipals for that reason for many decades. Except for certain "private activity" municipals under the 1986 tax law, the interest paid by municipals is exempt from federal income taxes. In many jurisdictions, it is also exempt from state and local taxes, if the buying individual resides in the place of issue.

But IRA owners already have tax advantage on interest from any source, whether otherwise taxable or not. *For IRA owners, municipal bond tax advantages mean nothing.* Municipals must therefore be evaluated side by side with other interest-bearing securities and savings instruments, for all these—when held by IRAs—are equally and greatly tax-advantaged.

Looking at it that way, you should realize that some high-quality municipals actually yield far less than many federally guaranteed deposits, federal bonds, and short-term money market funds—which are even safer. Other municipals are properly seen as extraordinarily risky, while still yielding less than some rather high-grade corporate bonds.

In pricing and interest rate terms, the problem is the relationship between risk and reward. Bond prices and yields tend to reflect the amount of risk involved, related to the after-tax yield of the bond; higher risks bring higher yields. But when you are dealing with a whole class of instruments—municipals—that are greatly tax-advantaged, prices and yields simply cannot be competitive when the tax advantage between all the kinds of bonds is equalized, as it is with IRAs.

For example, a very highly regarded municipal paying interest of only 6% may be worth a very competitive 10% to someone whose combined federal, state, and local income tax bracket adds up to 40%. That has been the attraction to wealthy individuals all along; indeed, in some periods of high top tax brackets, that 6% might have been worth an enormously attractive 30%, for someone in a combined 80% tax bracket. However, that 6% rate, paid into an IRA, is just 6% accreting tax-advantaged, and may be far less attractive than a federal bond accreting tax-advantaged at 8% to 11%. Similarly, a municipal paying 10% may look fine when compared with many much safer investments—until you realize just how risky most municipals paying that much interest really are.

Before the bottom dropped out of the equities markets in the early 1970s, municipals were almost exclusively sold to wealthy investors for their tax advantage. Then in the 1970s, municipals began to find wider markets, as brokers found small investors eager to put their money into instruments with high after-tax yields, which municipals certainly were. But what became clear after a few years was that those high after-tax municipal yields were the bond market's way of identifying large numbers of municipals as extremely risky investments, in a period of growing economic crisis for America's state and local governments.

That was driven home by the New York City bond interest moratoriums of the mid-1970s; the bondholders were unable to sell their New York City bonds at anything more than a small fraction of their previous worth. It was driven home even harder by such disasters as the Washington State nuclear energy bonds default of the early 1980s, in which tens of thousands of uninsured bondholders lost much of the half billion dollars they had invested in what were sold to them as high-quality municipals.

Since these disasters, more and more municipals have carried private insurance against interest moratoriums and outright defaults. That can be helpful in some situations, but it should be noted that municipal bond prices tend to drop sharply when such events occur, and there is no insurance against such price declines. Nor is it very likely that a truly massive default, as the New York City situation threatened to become but was not, and as the Washington State default actually became, will be adequately covered by its private insurance, no matter how large and well regarded the insurers. These are the kinds of liabilities that wipe out even the largest insurance companies, and insurers are quite likely to engage in years of litigation and setttlement of claims, rather than paying losses that would bankrupt them.

Types of Municipals

The safest kind of municipal is the *short-term tax anticipation note*, which is a borrowing by state and local government in anticipation of tax receipts coming later. These are used to smooth out revenue over a full year, as tax revenues tend to bunch with the time of year. They are issued in larger denominations than are practical for IRAs to buy, and so are mainly purchased by institutional investors and reached by individuals only indirectly, as part of mutual fund portfolios.

General municipal bond obligations, like equivalent federal obligations, are backed by tax revenues and carry a "full faith and credit" promise to pay. However, municipals issuers do not have unlimited taxing power, backed by the full force of the nation, as does Congress. Congress can and does create new money; we have seen that as the national debt has skyrocketed in these years. Municipals issuers cannot—but they can and do go effectively bankrupt—as we have also seen in these years.

Special assessment municipal bonds are backed by specific tax revenues, as when a bond is issued to finance a new addition to an existing sewer system, and the affected homeowners pay a special levy for some years to pay off the bond.

Revenue bonds are not backed by the taxing power of the state or local issuer, but rather by anticipated revenue flowing from the project being funded by the bond, such as an industrial park, shopping mall, or downtown renovation. These are the kinds of municipals that often pay the highest rates of all, for these are often also very risky indeed. That industrial park or shopping mall, virtually empty two years after completion, is a cash drain, rather than a revenue producer, and bondholders may in some cases reasonably anticipate moratoriums and defaults.

Note also that the tax advantages of municipals will now undergo further attack, as Congress seeks new sources of revenue. Note also—very carefully—that should municipal bond tax advantages be substantially further decreased, municipal bond issuers will be forced to offer much higher interest yields, to make up for lost after-tax yield advantages.

Should that happen, municipals now in existence will decline in value catastrophically, for their interest yields reflect their present tax advantage, and like all tradable bonds they will change in market value to reflect current interest conditions. That is inevitable if tax advantages diminish for these kinds of bonds; it is the way the worldwide bond market works. That possibility poses a very great hazard for municipal bondholders, whether they are holding as individuals, as self-directed IRA owners, or as mutual fund shareholders.

Municipal bond mutual funds spread the considerable risks involved in holding municipals. That can be a valuable function, in this very chancy section of the bond market, for those who do derive otherwise unavailable tax benefits from their ownership of municipals. But mutual funds provide no protection at all against the kinds of general declines that can occur when large bodies of investors become frightened after major municipal defaults, for then what is spread is both risk and general decline. Nor can such mutual funds protect at all against the kind of large general losses that would result from changes in the tax advantage rules.

In short, municipals should not be purchased for your IRA. They have no tax advantages, carry large intrinsic risks, and are subject to some major additional risks in this period.

Corporate Bonds

Not so long ago, the main American bond market was that of the corporate bond, and it was a slow-moving, very stable institutional market, with market and bond price moves measured in small fractions of percents, called *basis points*, each of them $1/100$ of a single percentage point. Today, with the enormous increases in federal, state, and local debts that have occurred in the 1970s and 1980s, the corporate bond market is far less important than before. It is also far more volatile, primarily because many major American corporations are far less stable and prosperous than they were in earlier decades, and also because low-quality corporate bonds have been very widely used as takeover funding vehicles in recent years.

That new situation in the corporate bond market creates new hazards; but it creates some substantial new opportunities, as well, especially for self-directed IRA owners who are willing to watch rather closely high-quality corporate bond yields. There is a good deal of relatively low-risk money to be made in high-quality corporate bonds by IRA owners. The yields are often much higher than those offered by any federal obligations, and both much higher and much safer than those offered by municipals.

There are really two quite different kinds of corporate debt obligations, one reachable only through mutual funds, the other accessible either by direct purchase or through mutual fund share purchases.

Short-term corporate debt obligations are part of the worldwide commercial paper market. Generally issued in denominations of $100,000 or more, these are 90- to 180-day obligations of major companies. Until recently, these were thought of as "blue chip" companies, but we are now in an era in which yesterday's blue chip may be today's bankruptcy. Even so, these are highly regarded obligations, actively purchased and traded by large institutional investors all over the world.

As highly rated and short-term as they are, they still tend to pay 1% to 2% more than federal short-term obligations, making many of them very desirable acquisitions for investment professionals running money market funds, company treasurers using them to soak up surplus cash, and other very large traders. There have been some defaults, though, in the increasingly troubled 1970s and 1980s, and investment professionals tend to trade in commercial paper rather more cautiously than they did in the boom years of the 1960s.

Individuals reach these short-term corporate obligations through mutual funds, especially money market mutual funds. So far, defaults have been so few as to pose no significant problem for such funds; they tend to diversify greatly, with such paper only a very small part of total holdings at any given time.

Medium- and long-term corporate bonds are entirely accessible to individuals and their IRAs. These are the debt obligations of privately owned companies, including industrial, financial, transportation, merchandising, and utilities companies of many sizes, conditions, and degrees of financial health. Like most of the government bonds previously discussed, they pay specified rates of interest and promise repayment of principal at a stated date, the *maturity date*. They are not guaranteed by any government; some may be privately insured for payment of interest and ultimate repayment of principal, though no insurance protects against price fluctuation before maturity.

A group of AAA-rated corporate bonds, paying in aggregate 2% more than medium- and long-term federal bonds, can be an excellent IRA investment, as the tax advantage lets that extra 2% compound freely, with the kinds of very beneficial results previously discussed. You can get at them directly, through a self-directed IRA, then paying transaction charges as you trade the bonds, or you can get at them indirectly through a bond fund, although that fund may mix lower-quality bonds with the higher-quality bonds you may really want to own.

When you do buy bonds directly—or for that matter, when evaluating how well a mutual fund is buying bonds on your behalf as a shareholder—you must be prepared to watch the progress of those bonds and of the companies issuing them, just as if they were common stocks, commodity futures, or any other kind of volatile investment. In today's markets, there are no "widows and orphans" securities—if there ever were. Bond values fluctuate greatly, in direct response to fluctuations in interest rates, bond rating revisions, and many other factors in the marketplace and the individual company.

You also have to know what you are buying, and how the nature of the bond may affect its chances of repayment. The most common kind of corporate bond is the essentially unsecured one, often called the *debenture* or *debenture bond*. This is a bare promise to pay, backed only by the "full faith and credit" of the issuer, and is only as good as its issuer. If that issuer is IBM, the promise to pay is likely to be good, even many years later, although you should certianly watch that bond as carefully as any other you buy. On the other hand, if that bare promise to pay is made by such a very troubled company as Union Carbide or Johns Manville, the bond may be a bad buy at any yield. Between these extremes, the bonds of other major companies have to be evaluated separately, with some requiring considerably higher yields than others, reflecting the market's evaluation of their relative safety.

A bond backed by some kind of collateral may often pay a little less than an unsecured bond of the same company but be a somewhat safer buy. Unsecured bonds are often subordinated to other debt claims, such as those of insurance companies and banks, rather than having first call upon company resources, and therefore may in a bankruptcy situation go into default even if some creditors are being paid in full. Bonds secured by collateral may have first call on that collateral, although a business failure may bring prolonged litigation between bondholders and creditors.

How good any bond is, including a collateralized bond, depends most of all upon how good its issuer is. The collateral can make a difference, but collateral owned by a going company is in most instances worth far more than collateral owned by a defunct one. That wonderful company headquarters or that huge plant securing a company bond issue are quite likely to turn into white elephants should the company go under.

Do not focus on the method the company is using to secure the bond with assets; the main things to determine are that the physical assets directly back the bond, and that the assets themselves will still be valuable should the company fail or stop operating those assets. That company headquarters may be worth nothing at all and be merely a cash drain if it is located in a small country area and cannot be resold. But if it is located in midtown New York City, it may be sitting on some of the world's most valuable commercial land; then it would be a major, wholly salable asset, and excellent collateral.

First mortgage bonds on land, or land and structures, that will hold their value may be very good collateral indeed. General mortgage bonds, however, are quite different. They are in essence second—or third or fourth—mortgages on property that is already mortgaged. For that reason, general mortgage bonds are seldom worth seeing as any safer than bonds carrying the bare promise to pay.

One special kind of corporate bond, which was popular in the boom years of the 1960s, is the *convertible bond*, so named because it gives its buyers the right to convert it into specified amounts of common stock, on terms specified by the bond's issuer on the bond itself.

The convertible bond pays a little less interest than a straightforward bond would; that is its main advantage for its issuer. For its buyers, it is a small speculation, for if the value of the preferred or common stock to which it is related rises enough, conversion at a profit will be possible and worthwhile. On the other hand, if the stock does not rise enough, some interest will be foregone, and the market value of the bond will probably also suffer somewhat. That is why convertibles become attractive in sharply rising markets, as in those of the mid-1960s and some portions of the early 1980s.

Junk Bonds

The early 1980s also saw the development of *junk bonds*, so named because that is exactly what they were and are. These are high-interest, low-quality corporate bonds, developed mainly to assist corporate raiders in their takeover attempts. Junk bonds are in net effect the debt obligations of corporations in seriously impaired financial positions, whether due to normal business reasons or because the whole process of corporate raiding terribly weakens the financial position of most corporations raided.

Do not buy junk bonds for your IRA, no matter how attractive their yields seem to be or how wonderfully they seem to compound out over the years on your computer. A junk bond at 17% is still a very poor risk. They pay that much because they are such bad risks, no matter what their promoters, packagers, and sellers say.

Do not buy mutual funds heavily invested in junk bonds, either. Their sellers may tell you that the rate of default on such bonds is very low, or at least low enough so that the very high interest rates paid on those that survive more than offset any failures. And that may be so, at the time you buy them—but it is not likely to remain so, for in a substantial recession, far short of a financial crisis, many of the badly damaged companies issuing junk bonds are quite likely to go into default, and many will fail. For some professional speculators, going in and out of junk bonds may be rewarding; all others should stay away from them.

Zero-Coupon Bonds

Zero-coupon bonds are a form into which bonds of several kinds are packaged and sold, rather than a debt obligation defined by the kind of issuer, as are federal government, municipal, and corporate bonds.

The basic device involved in creating zero-coupon bonds is literally dividing the bonds into two different kinds of securities, by stripping away their interest-bearing coupons, selling off the interest-bearing portions, usually in large denominations, and selling the remaining bonds at a deep discount to individual purchasers. Because these bonds are without their interest coupons, they sell at a small fraction of what they will pay at maturity, and are therefore often rather attractive to small investors, who are sold on the basis of receiving big, sure returns at maturity many years later. They have proven enormously profitable for their packagers, though how well they will work out for their purchasers very much remains to be seen.

For people purchasing these bonds with taxable money, there is a great tax disadvantage. The problem is that Congress decided some years ago to treat the eventual investment income from such securities as fully taxable interest year by year, as it is added to the value of the bond, even though bondholders do not collect such interest until many years later, when the bond matures. In the tax law this is *imputed interest*. The need to dig up cash for taxes every year, for gains you may not see for a generation, is properly considered a very great disadvantage indeed.

However, IRA owners need not worry about such taxes until they begin to pull money out of their IRAs, which takes most of the tax sting out of zero-coupon bonds for IRA owners. That is why zero coupon bonds are sold so hard as "ideal vehicles" for IRA money, because they cost so little at the start, pay so much on maturity, and are so safe and sure.

As is so often the case in the risky bazaar that is the modern financial marketplace, the truth is very, very different from what all those eager, not-always-so-scrupulous sellers tell you. Zero-coupon bonds are just bonds without their coupons, and their promise to pay at maturity is no better or worse than the same bonds from the same kinds of issuers *with* coupons. A federal guarantee is the same AAA guarantee, a corporate guarantee may still be anything from AAA to "stay away at all costs," and a municipal may still be anything from relatively safe to enormously risky. The private insurance guarantees may still be excellent in individual situations or worthless in the kind of major crisis we have not seen since such guarantees started being widely attached to securities of several kinds.

With or without their coupons, it is imprudent and entirely wrong to treat bonds (or any other kinds of investments) as if you could buy them, tuck them away, and not look at them again until maturity, for that way of doing your personal financial business courts disaster.

Actually, zero-coupon bonds are much, much riskier than ordinary interest-bearing bonds. That is because the price fluctuations of interest-bearing bonds, in response to changes in interest rates, are considerably lessened because of the presence of the promised interest payments. Zero-coupon bonds, without current interest payments, are terribly sensitive to interest rate changes. Because of the very low prices paid at the start for such zero-coupon bonds, even modest interest rate changes can mean quite large profits or losses relative to the cash money invested in them.

In this respect, then, they are in the early years of ownership highly speculative, rather than conservatively safe, bonds. Only near maturity, with most of their full maturity values near at hand, do they settle down and become the stable investments they are so often and so erroneously thought to be. At maturity—if they have lasted until maturity, rather than having been called (that is, retired early)—they pay stated sums; that is all that can be said to be safe and stable about them.

A stated rate of interest has to be related to the pace of inflation to become meaningful in real dollars. That you bought a zero-coupon bond for $100 in 1985, and will be compounding it for 30 years at 10%, until 2015, and will then have a magnificent $1,744 to show for it, doesn't mean a thing, unless inflation is less during that period. For if inflation averages 12% or so during that 30-year period, you will in real dollars have earned only a little more than half of what you will seem to have earned. And if current interest rates were higher than the rate at which your bonds were accumulating, and you wanted to sell your zero-coupon bonds before maturity, you might have to take a big loss. Indeed, you might decide in some circumstances to take that kind of heavy loss, rather than to hold on to what might then have turned into white elephants, yielding much less than what you might then make in other then-attractive investments.

Do not believe all this talk about tucking away some safe, high-yielding, zero-coupon bonds in your IRA portfolio. Their promises to pay are neither more nor less safe than the same bonds with their coupons still attached, and before maturity they are far more speculative than interest-bearing bonds. As we have discussed, some bonds may be superb IRA investments; buy them in their interest-bearing, rather than their zero-coupon, forms.

6

Asset-Backed Securities for IRAs

Asset-backed securities are a recent development in the American financial marketplace. They are essentially shares in pools of debt obligations, with the interest and repayment of principal of those obligations passed through the pool to those owning the securities, whether directly or through mutual funds. They are therefore also sometimes called *pass-through securities*. They are also called *mortgage-backed securities*, (even though that is only a partial description) because mortgages were the first instruments used to collateralize securities this way, and most of them are still backed by mortgages rather than other kinds of debt obligations.

In a sense, the phrase *asset-backed* is somewhat misleading, for the practice of backing promises to pay and repay with proper collateral has been long established. When a corporation issues a bond and collateralizes it by giving bondholders the right to come after specified property on default, the resulting bond is, in fact, asset-backed. When a lender advances money to a manufacturer who uses receivables as collateral, the resulting debt is asset-backed. Similarly, every mortgage is asset-backed, for the property itself collateralizes the promise to pay the mortgage loan.

When a government agency such as the Government National Mortgage Association (GNMA, or Ginnie Mae) buys mortgages from primary mortgage lenders, and resells them as standard-sized (usually $25,000) Ginnie Mae certificates, it has turned the mortgage loans into securities, thereby in financial jargon "securitizing" the mortgages, and created asset-backed securities.

When an investment banker or broker creates a pool of such Ginnie Maes and sells shares to the public—directly as shares, as shares in a mutual fund, or as shares in a unit trust, which is effectively a mutual fund form—then the existing asset-backed securities have been repackaged for ease of sale and the creation of commission income.

When an investment banker or broker takes existing debt obligations, such as long-term federal bonds or privately held automobile loans, and creates a pool of them to repackage and sell them in any of those forms, it is doing the "securitization" of the loans and creating the asset-backed securities.

Asset-backed securities might better have been called debt pool shares, for that is what they are. In principle, any pool of debts may be used to create and stand behind shares and mutual funds.

The modern development of these kinds of securities started when Congress decided to try to support an ailing homebuilding industry by developing a federally guaranteed secondary mortgage market. To that end, the Government National Mortgage Association created Ginnie Maes, which are federal agency issues that are directly and fully guaranteed by the federal government. Also to that end, the Federal National Mortgage Association (FNMA) created Fannie Maes, and the Federal Home Loan Mortgage Association (FHLMA) created Freddie Macs. The latter two are not directly federally guaranteed, being issued by privately owned organizations that are federally affiliated, but both main bond-rating agencies do, as of this writing, give them their highest ratings.

With the impetus provided by this federal creation of a new multi-billion-dollar market, others were encouraged to create similar mortgage-backed asset-based securities, some of them state and local government insured, some privately insured, some uninsured, and some not at all what they seemed to be.

Then, as the concept took hold in the financial marketplace, sellers began to create other kinds of asset-backed securities. Other federal agencies, such as the Small Business Administration (SBA), began to repackage their own loans, creating fully federally guaranteed medium-term asset-based securities to go along with the longer-term mortgage-backed securities. Other federally related but privately owned organizations, such as the Student National Marketing Association (Sallie Mae), also created such debt pool bonds.

Now, the concept is firmly established, and private organizations in many industries are creating many kinds of debt pool or asset-backed debt obligations, just as private organizations in the real estate industry created such obligations after the federal government led the way. Automobile loans are now packaged as asset-backed securities, with such organizations as the General Motors Acceptance Corporation and large banks creating billions of dollars' worth of debt pool shares out of their outstanding auto loans. Computer leases have also been so "securitized," while such receivables as credit card balances and large installment loans on such goods as boats and airplanes are quite likely to be turned into debt pool securities.

You can reasonably expect many other such securities to come to market, as well, for all public and private sector organizations carrying large pools of debt will be looking closely at this means of raising money, for it is a way to build much greater lending power. For hard-pressed public agencies, which cannot get more tax money to lend, this can be an enormously attractive device. For private lenders, and especially mortgagors and durable-goods sellers, the creation of new lending power can mean greatly enhanced sales and profits. And for bankers and brokers, this trend can be little less than a cornucopia, generating great profits and commissions as investment money flows into these debt pools.

For the country as a whole, of course, it means an expansion of the huge balloon of credit that already exists, and to some extent the pyramiding of debt upon debt, with additional layers of bankers and brokers taking profits from multiple transactions. This kind of pyramiding can have very serious consequences in a deep recession or depression.

To the individual investor with IRA funds to invest, it means that some attractive new federally guaranteed debt obligations have been created, with more to come. It also means that a great many not so very attractive obligations have been and will also be created. Some disasters have already happened in the mortgage-backed securities market; others will undoubtedly occur, as happens in every new, "hot" market. Where there is quick new money to be made, honest and competent financial people are inevitably joined by incompetents and thieves.

For the small investor, these asset-backed securities should be viewed as several new varieties of bonds and should be evaluated as IRA investment possibilities just as if they were bonds. Their yields are risk-related, their guarantees are as good as those making the guarantees, their collateral must be understood and carefully evaluated, and they are as sensitive to changes in interest rates as other, older kinds of debt obligations carrying similar risks and maturity dates.

The underlying attraction of the Ginnie Maes, Freddie Macs, Fannie Maes, Sallie Maes, SBAs, and all the other similar federal agency debt pools is that they are federally guaranteed or federally related, and pay a little more than do Treasury obligations of similar duration. Generally, that means half a point to a point more than comparable Treasuries. In the bond markets, that is expressed as 50 to 100 basis points, a basis point being $1/100$ of 1%.

For institutional buyers, 50 basis points—½%—makes such federally guaranteed obligations well worth buying in preference to Treasuries. For individuals, that may not be so, especially when transaction fees or mutual fund sales charges effectively wipe out some of the yield. Nor can small investors reach some of the main kinds of securities being offered in these markets; Ginnie Maes and Freddie Macs are issued in large denominations and accessible only through such investment-pooling devices as mutual funds and unit trusts. (This is not true of Fannie Maes and an increasing number of other federally guaranteed securities, which are being issued in small denominations.)

The net result is that most small investors in this part of the financial marketplace are buying fund shares promising much higher yields, some of them two or even three points above even long-term Treasury bonds. More on this in the chapter on mutual funds, but note here that yields and risks are related. The fund that advertises 12% returns on asset-backed securities, when new Ginnie Maes are paying 9%, is in all probability speculating in futures, risking some of its money in covered call options, taking high risks in repurchase agreements, and holding debts incurred at earlier high rates that may disappear when debtors renegotiate in a lower-rate environment.

Where risks are really similar, you can reasonably expect agency issues to pay a little more than Treasuries. That will be enough for many risk-averse IRA owners, who are likely to be quite satisfied to get somewhat higher yields with full federal guarantees; the only remaining risk will be bond market fluctuation.

You certainly can get much higher yields on some kinds of asset-backed securities than on the federally guaranteed agency securities. There are several kinds of mortgage and other debt pool securities available, in aggregate offering a wide range of returns and commensurate risks. Some pools are backed by collateral worth twice as much as the securities on offer, and also insured by groups of major private insurers.

These may be relatively safe, relatively high-yielding invest-ments, *as long as the collateral really is as stated*, and the insurers are major and well-established companies.

On the other hand, collateral may be badly overstated, and insurers may be so small as to make their guarantees worthless when real catastrophies occur. For example, the Bank of America suffered huge losses in the early 1980s when it turned out that mortgages backing some of its own securi-ties were nonexistent, and that the insurance company guar-anteeing those mortgages could not even come close to fulfilling its obligations. The Bank of America met its obliga-tions, and the losses were its own, rather than those of those who invested in these securities.

On the other hand, investors who bought the mortgage-backed securities of the Equity Programs Investment Corpo-ration were not as fortunate. The failure of that firm brought about the run on the Maryland state banking system that caused the largest bank holdiay since the Great Depression. There have been major mortgage-related failures elsewhere. Tens of thousands of Californians invested in high-yielding second mortgage pools that went bad when people walked away from homes they could no longer afford, having mort-gaged them so heavily that no equity at all was left.

In considering asset-backed securities, it is vital to realize that *normal investment rules apply*. What matters most here is the quality of the guarantee, the quality of the underlying pool of debts, and the quality and quantity of the collateral.

Note also that there are some state and lcoal debt asset-backed securities, which make them tax-advantaged munici-pals. For IRA owners, these are simply municipals, to be compared to other investments without the tax advantage factor. Like other municipals, they are not particularly appro-priate for IRAs, as those that are relatively safe will have yields much lower than those of comparable risks, while those offering higher yields will be commensurately risky.

You should not compare a high-risk pool of municipals with a much lower-risk pool of federally guaranteed agency obligations. Sellers of municipals make such comparisons, trying hard to sell their inappropriate securities as logical IRA investments, but they are not. In asset-backed securities, as in all securities, the right comparisons are yield to yield within comparable ranges of risk.

7

Stocks for IRAs

As IRAs become larger, and as interest rates dip, many IRA owners turn to the question of moving at least partly away from as-safe-as-possible debt instruments directly into shares of stock, or into mutual funds composed wholly or largely of shares of stock. That can be a relatively conservative and possibly rather lucrative course of action; it can also be a thoroughly imprudent and unsafe course of action. It all depends on how well you know what you are doing within the context provided by the markets of the time.

In principle there is nothing "right" or "wrong" about moving IRA money into stocks. Far from it. There can be times when interest rates are very low, share values are moving ahead rapidly, and some stocks are excellent investments.

Some stocks, that is; not "the market." For investment professionals managing billions of dollars' worth of funds, the several securities markets can indeed be seen as markets, with large numbers of diversified investments depending heavily on market trends, as well as on the specific securities invested in. But for small investors, "the market" is an abstraction. You don't invest in "the market," you invest directly in a specific company, or in many companies through a specific mutual fund, whether your investment is with taxable money or through your IRA.

Stocks in the 1980s

Many IRA owners in this period are moving seriously into stocks for the first time. Some may have had considerable involvement in buying stock directly and through mutual fund shares back in the 1960s, when small investors were hip deep in the exciting, booming stock markets of the time. But that was two decades ago, and since then a whole generation has grown up that knows very little about stocks and, until rather recently, has focused much more on safe-as-possible debt instruments, with some of the more adventurous going into high-risk speculations rather than stocks. However, the mid-1980s have seen a considerable revival of interest, as stocks and mutual funds composed of stocks have risen sharply; many small investors have moved back into the stock market, more through mutual funds than through direct purchase of stocks.

For those considering a move of some or all of their IRA money into stocks, it may be well worthwhile to review some stock and stock market basics, and to discuss briefly the underlying condition of these markets in this period. You cannot properly understand the risks and rewards involved in stock-based mutual funds without understanding the basic characteristics of the stocks composing those funds. Nor can you understand individual stock risks and rewards without a basic understanding of how stocks differ from other invest-ment opportunities.

It is easy to fool yourself and be fooled by others in the stock markets of the 1980s. The Dow Jones Industrial Aver-age is the most widely followed of all the averages; it is what most people mean when they say "the market." When that average rises to "historic highs," it is important to keep firmly in mind that *it is still worth at best a little more than half of what it was worth in the mid-1960s*. It hit 1,000 back then, and more than once—and that 1,000 was worth somewhere between 3,250 and 3,500 today, once you take into account the impact of inflation as measured by the Consumer Price Index. Historic highs, indeed; what nonsense.

Similarly, the mutual fund that advertises itself as having gained hundreds of percent in the last several years, or perhaps even more, may very well have done so. But it was done by investing in inherently risky, and therefore speculative, stocks; there is no other way to accomplish that, except in a prolonged boom based on huge real growth in the economy, as occurred in the early 1920s and the middle years of the 1960s. Even then, there must be some substantial element of speculation in such huge mutual fund gains.

Make no costly mistake about this period, though; it is most emphatically not a boom, and that is why "the market" is still worth only a fraction of what it was worth in the 1960s. This is a very troubled period for American business and its companies, characterized by huge bankruptcies and near-bankruptcies. Hundreds of banks have failed, with more to come, often because of what turned out to be bad loans to previously sound companies. We have seen an unprecedented corporate raiding movement, which has seriously weakened many otherwise solid companies. The all-important international balance of payments has turned very much against the United States, and we are a debtor nation for the first time in modern history. And our national debt now approaches the $2 trillion mark, a disaster we will all have to live with for decades.

No, this is scarcely a boom period; rather, it is a period requiring extreme caution when investing in the stock of American companies and mutual funds composed of such stock, for even yesterday's blue chip stock may no longer be so. However, it is also a period in which there is money to be made in stocks and stock-based mutual funds, as long as you watch your investments carefully and take great care not to lock yourself into mutual funds with front and back load charges that penalize for moving your money when you feel you should.

Some Basics

Deposits and bonds are loans, with you as lender, and with repayment and interest promised, usually at fixed but sometimes at variable rates. Many of them carry insurance guarantees, ranging from powerful federal guarantees to much less certain, but still often meaningful, private guarantees. Stocks make no such promises, are secured by nothing, and carry no insurance guarantees. They are purely and, in essence, quite simply ownership shares in private enterprises. Their owners are shareholders, stockholders, equity holders, who hope to profit from growth in company share values and also by sharing in any dividends declared by the company.

There are two kinds of stock—preferred and common. All stock votes, though that means little to small stockholders in major corporations, but preferred stock often has more voting rights than common stock, and is used by major owners for purposes of corporate control, as against raiders. Preferred stock gets stated dividends before common stock does, and often cumulates those dividends, meaning that if no dividends are paid in some years, they will be paid in future years along with the dividends of those future years, and all before common stock gets dividends.

For income protection, then, preferred stock is likely to be somewhat safer than the common stock of the same company. Common stock does get an unlimited share in dividends, though, rather than only stated amounts, and that can be a rather meaningful disadvantage for long-term holders of preferred stock in periods of inflation, for fixed dividends inevitably become worth less as the dollar becomes worth less. Common stock dividends tend to rise somewhat as inflation erodes the value of the dollar.

Most issued and traded stock is common stock, which shares company gains in a full and unlimited way. Not losses, though. You cannot lose more than the full value of your share of stock, should the company go broke and wind up actually owing more than it is worth. Company directors and officers may in some such situations be liable, but not common or preferred stockholders who are not directors or officers.

Common stock may be traded without restriction, though as a practical matter it can be freely traded only if there is a market for it. It is to create such a market and place a value on their stock that family-owned firms "go public"— that is, sell off some of their company ownership to the public in the form of stock.

The stocks that you are most likely to be trading in a self-directed IRA, and the stocks that mutual funds mainly invest in, are the stocks of large, widely held companies listed and traded on major stock exchanges in the United States and around the world, including the New York and American Stock Exchanges, several regional exchanges, and such major international exchanges as those in London and Tokyo. You also may be trading, to a lesser degree, in any of the many thousands of "over-the-counter" stocks that are not listed on major exchanges but are actively traded through a worldwide network of brokers in the over-the-counter market.

In today's computerized financial marketplace, it is very easy for an individual or institution anywhere in the world to place a buy or sell order with a broker, and for that broker to reach for and make a trade in a few minutes, through the huge computerized network that is the modern stock market.

As the world becomes smaller, there are also more and more foreign company stocks to buy, for small investors usually through mutual funds, rather than directly. You will be increasingly able to buy such stocks directly, but will continue to find it very difficult to assess the risks involved, as you are much better able to do with widely held American stocks.

For small investors, foreign stocks have extra hazards built into them, for it is exceedingly hard to guess at political, interest rate, currency, and home market conditions—all of which may greatly affect stock values—without the kind of continuous information and analysis that only investment professionals specializing in these areas can afford. In international investing, experienced mutual fund managers, with proven track records, can function to spread risks and move investment money from company to company and country to country in a timely way. Do not try to trade in foreign stocks—or, for that matter, in foreign securities or currencies—on your own.

Figuring Stock Yields

Yield is how much money a stock or any other investment makes for you. With ordinary taxable money, that is stated as *pre-tax* and *after-tax* yield, as the tax factors must be taken into account before you know how much you are making on sale. These tax factors are often very hard to figure in, because of such matters as the possible use of offsetting losses from current and previous years and changes in tax laws before sale. With IRA money, all this is much simpler, for the tax factors do not enter the picture. With IRAs, all dividends are reinvested, all profits are held, and all yield is after-tax.

Yield is always figured on an annualized basis; that is the only way to really know where you are, in comparison with other stocks and other kinds of investments. For example, you may buy a share of stock for $10. The stock pays no dividends while you own it, and you sell it exactly three months later for $10\frac{1}{2}$, or $10.50. You have made $0.50 on $10 in three months; projected out for a full year, that would be $2 on $10, or 20%. If you had lost the $0.50, you would have lost 20%, on the same "annualized" basis. Actually, you would have made a little less and lost a little more, once brokerage fees were taken into account.

More realistically—for there are few stocks you are likely to go in and out of that fast—assume that you buy the same share of stock for the same $10, and hold it for a year without selling it. In that year, it goes up $1, and pays dividends of $0.40 per share. The $1 is 10% on top of your original $10; the $0.40 is 4% more. You have gained $1.40, or 14%.

But note that only the $0.40 dividend is in cash. Until you sell that share of stock, the $1 you gained in stock value is only a "paper gain." Should the stock go down $1, you will have lost that seeming gain; should it go down $2, you will have lost 10% of your original investment.

With debt instruments such as bank deposits, your yield is the interest itself, for the instrument remains at its original value. With debt instruments such as negotiable bonds, your yield is the interest, though if you choose to sell, it will be interest plus or minus any change in the bond's market value from your time of purchase. With stocks, your yield is the gain in the value of the share itself, plus dividends, but only the dividends are certain until actual sale of that share of stock.

There is nothing at all certain about how stocks and stock averages will move, in the short or long term. That is what so many millions of small investors discovered to their sorrow when the booming stock markets of the 1960s became the deeply depressed markets of the 1970s. Because of their nature, stocks are intrinsically riskier than debt instruments of comparable quality, and you should therefore anticipate higher possibilities of reward before you go into them as a direct investor, through a self-directed IRA. Stock-based mutual funds—especially those composed largely of speculative stocks, of which more later—should also be seen as riskier than comparable debt instrument investments.

Cutting Direct Trading Costs

It is easy enough to trade stocks through a brokerage account, whether that account is an ordinary one or a self-directed IRA account. All you do is open the account, paying the necessary opening fee, and proceed to instruct your broker on the trades you wish to make, which will be executed in the normal course of stock brokerage business. You can tell a broker to buy or sell at the stock's price as of the time your trading instruction is received. You can direct that a purchase be made at any price up to a specified top price, or that a sale be made at any price down to a specified bottom price. And you can either place time restrictions on your order, making it good for any specified period, such as an hour or day, or make it good until you withdraw it.

The only operative way in which your self-directed IRA brokerage account differs from any other brokerage account is that the law prohibits you from using it to trade on margin—that is, with borrowed money.

The only financial way in which your self-directed IRA brokerage account differs from any other brokerage account is that it costs more to maintain—up to $50 for opening the account and up to $50 a year to maintain it, on top of normal transaction costs, of which more in a moment.

There, in those startup, maintenance, and transaction costs, lie substantial cost hazard and money-saving opportunity. For how you handle the cost of your self-directed brokerage IRA can make all the difference between excellent and mediocre return, and on the same transactions, handled with the same professional timeliness and skill. That is true for *all* small investor brokerage accounts, by the way, though for the IRA accounts a little more so than the ordinary accounts, because of the special startup and maintenance costs involved.

At present, there is fierce competition for accounts between "full commission" and "discount" brokerage firms throughout the financial industry. Big banks and other financial sellers, such as Sears, are also very much joining the battle. In most instances, the banks and other financial sellers have acquired or associated themselves with existing brokerage organizations, some full commission and some full discount. What is beginning to emerge, however, is a series of deeply discounted brokerage operations throughout the country, as more and more customers realize that they can get what they need through discount brokers, whether independent or allied with other financial firms, at half or less than half of what they have to pay full commission houses.

That's a fact, rather than just a comeon advertisement from a discount brokerage house. As of this writing, if you buy or sell—it doesn't matter which—100 shares at $50, a $5,000 transaction, a full commission broker will charge you somewhere in the neighborhood of $90 for making the trade. If you sell those 100 shares and then buy 100 other shares at the same price, making a normal shift of stocks within your portfolio, it will cost you about $180, which is a whopping 3.6% of the value of the money you have moved.

If you have a $25,000 self-directed IRA portfolio, and make just five such average sells and seven such average buys a year, a total of twelve transactions at $90 each, plus a $50 maintenance charge, you will wind up spending $1,130 on transaction costs that year. That's a small but profitable business for the broker—but an unnecessary and very real disaster for the buildup of your self-directed IRA fund. That $1,130 on $25,000 is a bit more than 4.25% a year, just for transaction costs, and may very well make the difference between a successful year and rather a poor one. You might have done better in debt instruments; even though lower yielding, they are safer and less expensive to hold and trade.

When you use a discount broker, the numbers become quite different. The $5,000 trade costs $35 to $50, rather than $90, while opening and maintenance costs will be small to nonexistent. And the larger the trade, the lower the cost, with transaction costs getting down to 30% or 40% of full commission transaction charges. Using the same example, total costs are in the $450 to $650 range, effectively about half what you would pay the full commission broker.

Some IRA owners will trade more often, and some less often; some in larger lots, some in smaller lots. The principle is the same; there is much to be saved by trading with a discount broker. Actually, the example above is loaded just a bit in favor of the full commission broker, as trades in lots of less than 100 shares, called *odd lot trades,* are normally even more expensive than 100-share or larger trades, called *round lot trades.* Recently, some large brokers have been lowering odd-lot trading charges to IRAs, though, and that trend should continue.

Note also that no small investor, including those who are IRA owners, can reasonably expect to get much in the way of investment analysis and insight out of any broker, including a large, full commission broker, although that is held out as an inducement by full commission brokers. That is nobody's fault; there just isn't enough commission income in it for a broker to consistently service such small accounts. At best, you will get an eager young account representative in your local brokerage branch, who every now and then calls to try to sell you whatever the firm is pushing that week, plus some newsletter and other mailed recommendations from the home office, which are no better or worse than you can buy for much less than you are paying in extra commissions. At worst, that eager young broker will sell you a totally inappropriate investment, and perhaps more than one, before moving on to greater affluence and larger accounts.

We are a long time away from the seasoned old customer's representative, who closely followed a limited number of securities, worked hand in glove with the firm's research department, and took particular delight in developing small accounts into big ones over the years. For financial savvy today, you must rely on your own developing skills, the sources of information you have learned to tap, and astute long-term financial advisers, not on brokers and other financial sellers.

Investment and Speculation in Stocks

There is certainly some money to be made—in some periods—in direct stock investment through a self-directed IRA.

At the same time, such investments should be made carefully, very selectively, without trying to outguess large institutional investors on short-term price swings. Avoid speculation with your IRA money, which is meant to be one of the center-pieces of your lifelong financial plan.

In some ways, today's stock market is more difficult for small investors than ever before, and that is so even when the market is going up. Many small investors have understood this, and have moved back into stocks mainly through mutual funds, rather than on their own. Largely, that is because this is not a booming market based upon a strongly growing economy, but rather a very nervous, erratic market, much affected by interest rate gyrations and even expectations about interest rate moves, and by the several other potentially very negative factors previously discussed.

When you buy a stock, you buy a piece of a company, and today it is harder than ever to know how that company and its stock value will move, unless you follow it very closely and know it very well, and in context within its industry. An oil or oil-related company may look wonderful today, using every standard investment analytical tool. Tomorrow, it may be the victim of a huge fall in world oil prices, brought about largely by international manipulation of oil supplies. A drop in real estate values may sink a seemingly sound financial ser-vices company, and some large, hitherto stable banks as well. A single disaster, occurring anywhere in the world, may sink or severely damage a huge chemical or pharmaceutical com-pany. All these things have happened, and recently.

Some small investors like to be quick in-and-outers in the stock market, and want to use their IRAs as a means of avoiding taxes on gains. That can be done, but it is just about the last thing you ought to do with IRA money, especially if you are a relative newcomer to stock market investing.

This kind of trading was never a particularly lucrative way for amateurs to go, for it puts them into direct competi-tion with investment professionals all over the world, while at the same time building up far more than ever the kinds of transaction costs recently discussed. Some not terribly scrupulous brokers like this sort of thing very much, and greatly encourage it, for it turns even small accounts into highly profitable ones. But for the small investors involved, all that results is increasingly dangerous speculation with smaller and smaller funds, as transaction costs and a few bad guesses eat away at limited resources.

Today, the advent of large-scale computerized trading makes it even more difficult for the small in-and-out investor to make money in direct stock trading. Large traders, especially some large brokerage firms, are now moving hundreds of millions of dollars in tandem with the popular stock market indexes, in an often successful attempt to make money on the spread between stocks and indexes. That results in very wide swings in some of the main market averages, and in some of the main stocks composing them, even in a single day. The small investor simply cannot compete short-term in that kind of market situation. You can, however, invest for medium- and long-term growth and dividends, even in these markets.

The Value of Familiar Companies

If you work for a large, publicly traded company, feel that you know it and its prospects well, and like what you see, by all means put some of your IRA money into it. Many early birds, working for such companies as IBM and Xerox way back when, became quite literally millionaires doing just that. No, not all your eggs in one basket, and not if the company is so thinly traded that it is not listed on a major exchange. But certainly if it is widely enough held and traded, you have other investments, and you feel you know enough. If you don't feel you know enough about your own company, it is easy enough to learn. Company managements usually go far out of their way to make it easy for employees to learn about and invest in the company's future.

Similarly, some companies in your own industry or trade may be very attractive. The highly successful competing company, the supplier you come to know a good deal about, the longtime bellwether company in the industry—all these you can learn a good deal about through trade sources. More than that, you will understand their performance and prospects far better than those of companies in unfamiliar industries. It may require some reading, some asking, some rather careful research in the kinds of sources previously discussed, but that kind of work is well worthwhile. For small investors today, it is far better to come to know a good deal about a few companies in a few industries, or even in one industry, than to try to become an amateur expert and stock speculator, with or without the help of some friendly broker.

Similarly again, there are some large companies in growing and centrally important industries that are still properly regarded as "blue chips," and are proper investments for that most important long-term IRA money. For example, short of economic catastrophe, accompanied by a total change in social system, you are not very likely to see any huge drop in the value of something like IBM or AT&T stock. Even selling high in any given period, such stocks offer a very attractive combination of dividends and growth, both accumulating entirely tax-free for IRAs.

It is probably wise to avoid the hard-hit basic industries, such as steel, though; even if they seem attractively underpriced at any given time, they are quite likely to continue to be terribly troubled, with today's seeming assets melting away. Similarly, the accident-vulnerable chemical industry scarcely seems a very good prospect for long-term IRA money.

But all this is a matter of taking a close look when you are ready to invest; no specific recommendations are being made here, even though it is tempting to do so, for the times move too quickly for a book to be the right vehicle for specific recommendations. By the same token, it is wise to bear in mind that even though you may be putting your IRA money into long-term stocks, you will not then be "tucking those stocks away." Far from it. No investment should be tucked away. Every investment should be watched rather carefully all the time; at least once a year you should take a long, searching look at everything you have.

8

Annuities for IRAs

Annuities are primarily tax advantage devices, which lose a good deal of their appeal when considered as possible investments for already tax-advantaged IRAs. When you buy an annuity, you are buying into an investment fund in the form of a life insurance contract. Your contributions to and ultimate payouts from that fund depend upon the annuity you select, and the contract also provides for payout to your stated beneficiaries should you die before the term of the annuity has run.

An annuity purchased with taxable income is being purchased with after-tax income, which then builds tax-free until ultimate payout. An annuity purchased with IRA money is tax-deductible up to legal IRA limits, and then builds tax-free until payout. The great attraction of annuities is precisely that tax-free buildup, which is so tremendously advantageous in the long run. When purchased with IRA money, that advantage disappears, for the IRA itself is just as tax-advantaged as the annuity.

Therefore, if you are going to have more to invest than you can legally put into an IRA, it makes sense to use your IRA for investments other than annuities, which would otherwise not be tax-sheltered, and use annuities to create further tax shelter. On the other hand, if your IRA is your main long-term investment vehicle, an annuity investment can be considered along with all other IRA alternatives. It must be considered without its otherwise important tax advantages, though, just as you view such other tax-advantaged investments as municipals.

Seen that way, annuities are generally not terribly attractive IRA investments. They tend to do only a little better than comparable federal debt issues, and they carry back-load charges that make them less attractive than some very conservatively managed no-load mutual funds that pay just as well. They may also carry fixed interest guarantees for a year or longer, which may in some instances cause their managers to invest rather too speculatively; that is what happened in the celebrated Baldwin-United situation, which gave annuities a bad name for quite some time. However, they are sold hard and very successfully as IRA investments, and that alone should cause them to be covered in this book.

It is important first to distinguish competitive modern annuities from the older annuity contracts, many of which are still in existence. Modern annuities pay competitive rates of interest, carry back-load but hardly ever front-load charges, and are essentially liquid. The older annuities paid absurdly low rates of interest to their unfortunate owners, 2% to 4%, usually carried large front-loaded insurance sales charges, and were often quite illiquid. The older annuities made insurance companies rich, as yields from their investment portfolios far outstripped those tiny 2% to 4% interest rates they paid for the use of annuity money. Conversely, they made their owners far poorer than they should have been, as inflation sharply cut the value of the eventual annuity payouts. When you buy a modern annuity, you can reasonably expect that instrument to relate to current interest and inflation rates.

Annuity contracts today come in two basic forms, although there are several different selling names attached to those forms. The first of these is the *deferred annuity*, which is often described by the way investment contributions are paid by policyholders. For example, when a single large contribution funds the whole annuity, it is called a *single-premium deferred annuity.* When contributions to your annuity fund can be made at any time, which would be more the case in most IRA annuity situations, it may be called a *flexible-premium deferred annuity.* In either case, the payments you make to the annuity investment fund grow and compound in the years to payout.

The insurance company guarantees a specified rate of return on the annuity fund. That rate is changed periodically, usually yearly, but in some contracts it is guaranteed for as long as four or five years. Where the rate is changed yearly, you can expect half a point to a point more than comparable term Treasury issues, though not necessarily more than comparable term federally guaranteed agency issues. Where the rate is guaranteed for periods longer than a year, it is likely to be guaranteed for as little as comparable Treasury issues themselves are yielding as of the time of sale of the annuity.

The longer-term guarantees are questionable, though; should interest rates decline sharply, the guarantees will either not be met because the money will just not be there or be met by the use of increasingly risky investment management practices. The one-year guarantee is enough, and it usually carries with it the ability to pull your money out of the annuity without back-load charges if the guarantee drops beyond a certain level in any succeeding year. For example, a guarantee of 9% may carry a "bailout rate" of 7%, meaning that if the guaranteed rate goes below 7% next year you can pull your money out of the annuity fund without additional charges.

There are also insurance companies offering annuities that tie interest payouts to specified indexes, much as flexible rate mortgages do. An annuity fund offering three points more than the one-year Treasury bills rate would pay 9% when that rate was at 6%, and go down a point when the Treasury rate went down a point.

Few deferred annuities carry front-load sales charges, although most do carry back-load charges; for instance, such charges may start at 7% in the year of the annuity purchase and go down 1% each year until there are no charges for withdrawals after seven years. Should the annuity owner die before the annuity matures, back-load sales charges are waived. Most contracts also provide for withdrawals of up to 10% each year without back-load charges.

The other kind of modern annuity is the *variable annuity*. This annuity contract creates a straightforward investment fund, in which the value of the annuity depends upon how well the investments in it do. The annuity owner picks the kinds of investments the annuity will buy, choosing usually from several stock, bond, and money market funds offered by the insurance company, or may choose to go into Treasury issues, and can move from investment to investment several times each year without charge. These arrangements are much like those available when you invest in a family of mutual funds.

Front-load charges seldom accompany variable annuities, but several other kinds of charges can be involved. There are back-load charges, which in many instances are a full 10% for all withdrawals made during the first ten years, then dropping off completely. There are sometimes money withdrawal restrictions. There are also investment management fees, usually running 1/2% to 3/4% annually; additional annual administrative charges; a variety of legal and other miscellaneous fees that may go as high as 1% more annually; and as much as 1 1/2% additional each year for mortality experience deductions, for many annuity holders are living longer than earlier actuarial predictions had indicated, with consequently greater payouts from insurance companies on some annuity policies.

Only the back-load charges are fixed by the terms of the annuity contract; all the costs may go up during the life of the contract. Note that the mortality experience deduction may indeed go up a good deal in the decades ahead, for insurance company mortality tables have had to be revised again and again as average lives have greatly lengthened.

All these charges, so many of them quite open to increase, make the variable annuity contract rather questionable as an IRA funds vehicle. If you want to move some of your IRA money in the direction of this kind of family of funds, you can do so by investing in a no-load group of funds, without back loads, administrative and miscellaneous fees, or large mortality fee deductions. For the investment management being delivered, most companies offering variable annuities are charging far more than comparable no-load mutual funds, and usually in aggregate considerably more than even front-loaded mutual funds.

Once the tax advantage is put aside, as it must be for already tax-advantaged IRAs, there is little point in buying variable annuities with IRA money. If you want to move some or all of your money into annuities, it is better to buy a deferred annuity.

When you buy annuities, or for that matter any other kinds of insurance contracts, be very careful to buy from either a very large national company or from a smaller company licensed to do business in a highly regulated state such as New York or Pennsylvania. An insurer's promise to pay is only as good as the established strength and financial reserves of its maker. Note also that any company offering you much better annuity interest promises than those offered by other companies may be in considerable difficulty not so very far down the line. The only way to come through on imprudently made fixed-interest annuity promises, in a market characterized by falling interest rates, is to take imprudent risks with the annuity holders' money; and that way lies disaster.

If you buy an annuity, it is wise to be satisfied with interest guarantees on the high side of whatever is the going rate for such annuities, while carefully watching sales and other charges.

9

Mutual Funds for IRAs

In today's financial marketplace, there seem to be at least three dozen different ways of investing your money, each of them pushed by eager sellers as a source of prosperity now and a long, long life in the sun later on. As we have seen, some of these investment vehicles are not legal for IRAs, and others are inappropriate because the tax advantages of IRAs negate the otherwise special tax appeal of those kinds of investments. But there still are a great many different investment forms pushed as "ideal" for IRA owners, so many that their very variety can be a source of considerable confusion and investment error.

They are not that new. Almost every investment form legal for IRAs has been out there for at least a decade or two, and even the newer forms tend to be adaptations of much older techniques. There really aren't very many ways to invest your IRA money. You can loan your money to a bank, for interest, in a demand or time deposit. You can loan your money directly to a borrower, for interest and in some instances for trading gain; that is a direct purchase of a bond or other debt instrument. You can buy a direct share in an enterprise in the form of stock or a partnership interest.

You can also do any or several of those by pooling your money with other investors, in any of the dozen or so professionally managed mutual fund, unit investment trust, morgage-backed security, limited partnership, and annuity forms now being sold to investors, or for that matter through the traditional investment club, in which you pool money with other investors in a self-managed investment fund. Yes, there are a few new investment forms today, but the main development has been the creative packaging of old forms by investment sellers, often to their very great financial advantage.

Mutual Funds and Their Charges

The main pooled investment form in use today is the *mutual fund*, which is an investment company organized for the sole purpose of investing the money of others. When you buy shares in a mutual fund, you are buying into that investment company, just as when you buy shares of stock, you are buying into a single enterprise. Here it is the investment company itself that is the enterprise, with the market value of each of your shares at any given time equaling essentially the total value of the investments in the mutual fund divided by the number of shares outstanding. In this ownership respect, all mutual funds are the same, for whatever investment purposes they are organized.

They are all the same in another respect, as well (as are all pools of investments managed by professionals for investors): they require payment for professional management of your money. For there is no way at all to get around the fact that, in one way or another, you are going to have to pay for this management, no matter how well that fact may be hidden or disguised by investment sellers. And that is perfectly reasonable—as long as what you pay is reasonable, and the least you need to pay to secure that professional management. That a mutual fund management charges you a little more or less than $1/2\%$ per year for managing your investment is entirely to be expected; it's a small enough fee if the fund is well managed. That is a perfectly legitimate kind of charge, and indeed rather low, as these things go. If you have to pay $3/4\%$ per year for investment management, that is also entirely within an acceptable range of charges.

It is much more complicated than that, however. In these years, the amounts pulled out of investment pools by their promoters, managers, and sellers vary tremendously, and often without any relation at all to the services being rendered. Large amounts of money can be lost by the unwary, and large amounts saved by the knowing.

One mutual fund may charge an $8^1/2\%$ startup sales fee, plus $3/4\%$ yearly. Another may charge nothing at the start, but a real 2% a year in combined management and sales charges (which amounts to much more) for long-term fund shareholders. A third fund may charge nothing at the start, a moderate management percentage fee yearly, but charge a big 5% if you sell your shares within the first several years of ownership. A fourth fund, just as good in every investment way as the others, may charge only a modest yearly management percentage fee.

Similarly, but much harder to determine without extremely careful scrutiny of prospectuses, a real estate organization may skim 10% to 30% off the top of an offering before selling to investors at full price. Or a unit trust may offer a very nice-looking package of bonds with small management charges, but take its healthy cut of your money for putting the bond package together.

In the mutual fund area, some published help is available when it comes to determining the real charges levied by the funds in which you might want to invest. Wiesenberger, Lipper, and several other investment publishers offer a considerable range of books and services, which include information on management fees and sales charges. And *Forbes* magazine, which is in many libraries, publishes an excellent yearly summary of mutual fund performance that gives a very clear look at real charges.

Significantly, the *Forbes* summary makes it completely clear that *there is absolutely no relationship at all between fees and performance*. Many of the best performing funds in the country charge nothing but modest yearly management fees, and some of the worst charge very high total fees. The opposite is also so; some of the worst charge little, and some of the best charge much. There is simply no relationship between performance and fees, which makes it obvious that it pays to take the trouble to find funds that do well and charge little.

It may be helpful to discuss the main terms and charging techniques you will encounter when buying into such investment pools as mutual funds, unit trusts, and annuities.

Front load. A sales charge, or for that matter any charge levied by a seller, that is subtracted at the start from the sum invested, with the remainder treated as the amount actually invested. It is common in selling mutual fund real estate, asset-backed securities, limited partnerships, and life insurance. Mutual fund front loads may run as high as 8½% of the sum invested.

Many funds charge such very high front loads, and such charges can very significantly and negatively affect both your mutual fund investment yields and your vitally important investment flexibility. For example, assume that you buy $100 worth of mutual fund shares carrying an 8½% front load, which is the normal amount levied by most front-loaded funds. At the moment the transaction is consummated, you have only $91.50 worth of mutual fund shares, having lost $8.50 of your investment money by the act of buying into the fund. If you wanted to sell your shares the next day, and their value had not changed since the moment of purchase, all you would get would be that $91.50.

If on the other hand you hold onto your shares, the loss caused by the front load charge will have a terrible effect on your yield in the first year of ownership and indirectly beyond, as well. For if you buy for $100, get $91.50, and gain a respectable 11% that year, you end the year with $101.56, minus whatever modest management fee is being charged. That amounts to a gain of less than 1%—indeed a terrible rate of return. But if you had bought $100 worth of mutual fund shares for your $100, you would have gained the full 11%—and would have started the next year of ownership on a compounding base of $111, rather than from $101. If the shares went down, the situation would be even worse; any loss is greatly magnified, for you have lost a good deal to start with, and loss then builds upon loss.

In a way, what is even worse is that the existence of the instant loss of $8\frac{1}{2}$% at the moment of purchase all too often acts as a bar to your taking effective, timely trading action. You may have bought into a group of funds, which allows you to move your money without additional charge from fund to fund, and therefore be able to move in that way freely. But if you want to move your money out of a fund or that group of funds altogether, the front-load charge loss is very real, and may cause you to hold, rather than move.

That kind of front-load-entrapped holding is precisely what it is wise to avoid, as so many mutual fund shareholders found when the bottom dropped out of the stock market in the early 1970s. When a whole set of markets declines, so can a whole set of mutual funds; some go down more than others, but all go down.

Back load. A charge—sometimes a very large 5% to 7%—for selling your mutual fund or other investment pool share. This charge usually disappears entirely after a stated number of years, sometimes starting to drop off two to three years after purchase and continuing to drop point by point until no charge at all is levied on sale five to seven years after purchase.

Back loads are usually presented by sellers as being not as onerous as front loads, in that your money compounds fully on purchase and in subsequent years of shareholding, rather than suffering that big instant loss on purchase that accompanies front-load charges. Sellers also often tell the credulous that since they are "in for the long haul anyway," the back-load charge has no effect at all, because it drops down and then off as the years go by.

Yet, the fact is that in one important way back loads are just as damaging as front loads: they cause investors to hold on when they should be selling. Thus they may also cost even more in total dollars paid to the seller than seemingly higher front-load costs. Consider what might happen should you sell, several years after purchase, mutual funds or other investment pool shares bought for $100 with all your gains and distributions held and reinvested, which is most likely to be the case in your IRA. Four years after purchase of a successful fund, with compounding beginning to seriously work for you, your $100 might have grown between to $160 and $200, or perhaps even more. An 8½% front-load charge at the start would have cost you $8.50. But a 7% back-load charge on sale of shares worth even $180 would cost you $12.60, nearly half again as much.

What can happen when you confront those kinds of charges is a kind of paralysis. You may know very well that it is time to sell, such as in a market that is very clearly headed down, and perhaps far down. On the other hand, there can be a tendency to wait "just one more year," until the back-load charge drops off. But in investment, timing is everything; that paralyzed wait while you try to save on back-load charges can cost you a great deal more than the charges would.

Minimize back-load charges just as assiduously as you minimize front-load charges. As long as there are excellent no-load funds available, which require neither, buy them. If there comes a time when such excellent no-load funds are no longer available, then look hard for the lowest-load funds you can find. No matter what any seller tells you, there is absolutely no difference in professional performance between funds that charge high fees and funds that charge low fees.

Distribution fees. Some sellers, including some of the

largest securities houses in the country, very carefully hide their high fees in their prospectuses, calling them "distribution fees" or whatever else sounds as routine and innocuous as possible. These sellers will charge you an entirely acceptable 1/2% or 3/4% for professional investment management, and then add on entirely unacceptable charges of up to 1 1/4% more every year. The net effect of this is to build up total charges that for medium- and long-term shareholders are much higher than either front- or back-load charges.

These charges are often hidden rather skillfully, so much so that those charging them sometimes even call them "no-load" funds, selling them to investors who think they are successfully avoiding unacceptable charges.

Low load. There is growing resistance to all these charges, as increasingly sophisticated small investors seek out true no-load funds. As a direct result, some sellers have trimmed their charges and are able to call their offerings low-load funds. Some really are lower than they used to be, but beware the formerly high front-load seller who turns up with low loads front and back but high distribution fees buried somewhere in the prospectus. What sellers have learned in this fund area is that millions of investors continue to be startlingly unaware of the existence of excellent, truly low-cost funds, and quite willing to innocently and trustingly take the advice of their friendly brokers.

No load. No load means *no load.* Not low load; not hidden charges, in the form of distribution fees. Just professional investment management fees, in the range of 1/2% to 3/4%. And if somebody running a successful fund wants to charge you a full 1% for investment management, that should be all right with you, too.

That investors continue to pay wholly unnecessary high fees for the privilege of buying funds that are no better than real no-load funds is purely and simply a triumph of the sellers' art. In fact, all you have to do to get a list of no-load funds is to ask such discount brokers as Charles Schwab or

Quick and Reilly. Then all you need do is check the standard mutual fund services and handbooks mentioned earlier for previous fund performance, call for prospectuses and selling material, and make your decisions. You can certainly also talk funds over with your financial advisers and others, such as brokers.

In any discussion with financial sellers, though, be aware that funds charging high sales and "distribution" fees generally pay much better commissions to sellers than do true no-load funds. This is part of what those high fees are all about. That is also why roughly two-thirds of all mutual fund sales continue to carry significant sales charges, for the overwhelming majority of securities sellers push what pays them best. That may or may not be particularly ethical, but it is certainly not illegal and is surely predictable. In this matter, as in all other matters in the financial marketplace, you have to protect yourself, and should not expect anyone else to do that part of the investing and financial planning job for you.

Assessing Funds

The Track Record Question

When you buy a mutual fund, the essence of what you are buying is the quality of that fund's professional investment management. That is so whether you are buying a piece of a bundle of rather safe short-term debt obligations or of a bundle of highly speculative stocks. Different fund managments' investment in the same kinds of securities can and do come up with vastly different results; you need only study the excellent annual *Forbes* roundup of fund performances to see that.

That being so, it becomes vital to see how well funds have done before you invest in them, and you can only do that successfully if you have some specific fund history to study.

Finding that history is easy enough, in the fund prospectus, and in the standard services and handbooks; but if there is no real history, there is nothing to study.

A fund that is a startup situation, with little or no assets, is merely a blind pool of assets—including yours if you invest—whose managers may or may not do as well as they claim to have done with other funds. A fund that is a year old, and shows magnificent yield in that year, may also be one that some astute promoters have started rather low and built rather fast, to lure the unwary. A fund composed of "hot" speculative stocks in a booming speculative stock market may show several years of extraordinary growth, far outperforming the stock averages, but that fund is likely to come down fast when that whole market comes down, as it inevitably must. If you buy that speculative fund very low, at the start, and sell high, before a prolonged market downturn, you may do very well. If you buy after all that super-performance, and then hold too long, when the market goes down and the fund goes down faster, you may lose your shirt.

Prudence demands that you seek out funds with track records that reach through some long-term market ups and downs, with histories that go back beyond even a prolonged upturn. Prudence further demands that you avoid the fund with too little history for you to be able to make a reasoned decision. Prudence clamors that you not invest in a blind pool of money no matter how well other investments run by the same managers have done. Find excellently run no-load funds with excellent long-term track records; they are there.

The Question of Diversification

There are two significant possible benefits stemming from mutual fund ownership. The first, already discussed, is professional investment management. The second is that lower total risks may result from the spreading of risk that occurs when you buy a share of a diversified mutual fund portfolio, rather than investing in a small number of shares and debt obligations.

The seller's argument is that if you own five different stocks, and one or two of them do very badly, you may be hard hit. If you own a share in a mutual fund that owns the stocks of 50 companies, watching all of them and moving money out of them into better risks in a timely way, you are far less likely to get into trouble. Similarly, those owning bonds that are not fully federally guaranteed may be more vulnerable to individual bond defaults than those owning shares in pools of bonds, whether those pools are in funds that move in and out of many kinds of bonds or in unit trusts, which invest in a fixed and stated pool of bonds.

There certainly are such benefits to be derived from diversification, especially for small investors, who cannot meaningfully spread their limited funds over a great many different kinds of risks, and are in fact often penalized by the proportionally higher transaction fees charged for small transactions. A large, diversified, stable mutual fund with an excellent track record can offer considerably less risk than a small number of investments of the same kind as those in the fund.

On the other hand, it does not do to accept selling talk about diversification too uncritically. Someone who tries to sell you shares in a junk bond fund is selling you many high risks, instead of a few, and often profiting handsomely by doing so. Someone who tries to sell you shares in a municipal bond fund that is trying hard to surmount its intrinsically low returns by investing in some very high-risk municipals is lulling you to sleep with talk of diversification, while actually selling you a pool of very high-risk bonds.

Similarly, diversification helps little when all or most of the stocks in a high-flying "aggressive growth"stock fund go down together in a prolonged market slump, as happened in the early 1970s. Nor does it help when a "special purpose" fund invested heavily in oil stocks is devastated by a fast, unanticipated decline in world oil prices, or a gold mining stock special purpose fund is hit by a sharp decline in gold prices. Nor will it do much good if a new tax law takes away so many municipal bond tax advantages that municipals issuers have to pay much more interest than before to attract buyers for their bonds, thereby forcing down the values of billions of dollars' worth of existing municipals. Certainly, diversification of risk can be a good thing, when investing in comparables, but only to cushion the impact of individual stock declines and debt issue declines and defaults.

The Question of Insurance

In recent years, the great number of bank failures, junk bond defaults, threatened municipal bond defaults, second mortgage fund failures, limited partnership failures, and the like have made investors extremely and quite properly cautious about the quality of payment promises. That is the underlying reason that so many IRA owners are risk-averse, preferring to put their money in federally insured CDs and into funds they believe to be fully federally guaranteed—although many of the latter are not so safe and so guaranteed as their promoters make them seem.

In response to that caution, many public and private debt issuers have secured private insurance of the interest and payout-at-maturity promises of their bonds and bond funds, thereby gaining both credibility in the marketplace and coveted high ratings. The insurer makes no guarantees as to the market value of the bonds during their lifetimes, but does make full guarantees on payment of interest and principal, undertaking to pay all sums due in timely fashion in any default situation.

Private insurance can be a meaningful lessening of risk in individual default situations, as when a single small or medium-sized issuer defaults. But private insurance is not federal insurance, and no private insurer or group of insurers will be able to withstand truly masssive defaults, whether they are those of a single major city, a single huge corporation, a single big power authority, or a larger group of corporate or municipal issuers. Private insurance should be taken seriously, and treated as a plus when it is coming from a group of very large national insurance companies, but it should never be equated with the far more reliable federal guarantees. You must still look at the underlying quality of the debt obligations carried in a mutual fund portfolio, and make quality the main ingredient of a buying decision.

Open-End and Closed-End Funds

Mutual funds are organized in two standard forms, the *open-end fund* and the *closed-end fund*. The open-end fund, by far the more prevalent, is the kind of fund you are most likely to buy into. The closed-end fund is far less popular in this period.

The open-end mutual fund is one that is organized to continue to sell new shares to the public, continuously investing new share money along with existing fund capital. Each new share so created is exactly equal to all other existing shares as of the time of sale, and from then on participates in all gains, losses, and distributions. Most mutual funds are organized along these lines, and those who sell you mutual funds will almost always be selling open-end funds.

There is a wrinkle, though: some open-end funds will suspend new sales for certain periods, even for years. That most often occurs when a fund—particularly a special purpose or speculative fund—has been doing extremely well, and its management fears that not enough excellent investment opportunities of the kind it normally seeks are available to put new share money into. That does not mean converting the fund into a closed-end fund, though, for that is an entirely different matter. The fund is still open-end in form, and the assumption is that it will resume new share sales at a later time.

That, of course, creates another kind of wrinkle, for fund managements rarely want to stop selling new shares altogether. The usual solution is to create new funds, selling them on the basis of the excellent track record of the fund whose sales have been temporarily closed. Investors who do buy such new funds may indeed thereby secure the same kind of excellent management that made earlier funds do so well. But it is wise to consider each new fund as only that—a new fund with promise but without a track record—and to be wary of investing in it until it has developed some history.

Closed-end funds are much more like operating corporations with fixed numbers of shares outstanding, which are traded in the open market. They are pools of investment money, like other mutual funds, but are organized with a specific number of shares: sales of new shares do not proceed indefinitely, or as long as someone is willing to buy. When you buy into a closed-end fund, you buy a share on the open market, a traded share that someone else has sold. When making a buying decision, you look for essentially the same proven track record and goals compatibility that you seek with any mutual fund.

Unit Trusts

The *unit trust* is a specific variation on the closed-end fund. It has become fairly popular in the United States only recently, although it has been in use in Great Britain for many years.

Unit trusts are pools of specific debt instruments, usually specific bonds, which are packaged by securities houses into fixed large funds and sold off to investors in small quantities. When you buy into a unit trust, you buy a piece of the pool, drawing a share of interest and principal repayment commensurate with your share of total trust holdings. Your payout is specified on purchase, and in these years is often guaranteed by private insurance of the bonds being held.

On the other hand, these are tradable bonds, which as

every prospectus makes clear may fluctuate in price over the years. And they will, of course; that is their nature. What you must consider beyond any insurance guarantees, therefore, is the underlying quality of the bonds in the portfolio. You should not assume that you are going to tuck away your unit trust shares, any more than you will tuck away any other securities. You may want to sell before maturity for any of a score of personal or investment reasons, and you want good-quality bonds that may have appreciated in value by then, rather than poor-quality bonds that may have lost much of their value. In a unit trust, those bonds diversify your bond-holdings; but the quality of the bonds is still the main question to address when making a buying decision.

Kinds of Mutual Funds

There are now as many different kinds of mutual funds available as there were in the roaring 1960s, and some more besides. The mutual funds portion of the securities industry has prospered greatly in the middle 1980s, and the result has been a huge proliferation of funds and kinds of funds. At this writing there are almost 1,500 funds to choose from: money market funds; stock-based funds of many kinds and for many purposes; bond funds of several kinds, including some quite recently developed that are based upon new financial instruments; old reliable balanced funds; international funds; index funds; timing funds; and a good deal more. There are funds organized to reach for aggressive growth at high risk, moderate growth at moderate risk, and income production at low risk. Today there are even funds of funds again, with the potential of not one but two layers of management and sales fees—shades of the 1960s.

Here are the main kinds of funds that you may find yourself considering for IRA investment. Most are reasonably possible investment vehicles for IRAs; their suitability depends upon your goals, their long-term track records and recent track records as of the time you might buy them, and the possible availability of more attractive alternatives. A few are included not because of their intrinsic usefulness as IRA investments, but rather because they are being sold hard when they are in fact questionable for IRAs.

Money Market Funds

In form, money market funds are mutual funds. Like all mutual funds, they are pools of investment money put into the hands of investment professionals, who for a fee manage the pooled money. In fact, money market mutual funds are, by their nature, more like savings accounts in very conservatively managed banking institutions than anything else, even though the funds are neither classified as banking institutions nor insured by any agency of government.

Money market funds invest in short-term instruments of several kinds. By law, they may not invest in instruments maturing in more than one year; in practice, they seldom invest in instruments maturing in more than three months, and much of their investment is in instruments maturing much faster than that. They are mostly the kinds of very large short-term obligations that have long been traded all over the world by institutions and a few wealthy individuals, such as U.S. Treasury bills, $100,000 bank certificates of deposit, and a wide range of commercial paper, essentially the short-term IOUs of major corporations.

There are three kinds of money market funds, all of them investing in short-term financial instruments. The first is the general money market fund, which invests in the full range of short-term instruments, including the debt obligations of federal, state, and local, corporate, and financial and banking issuers.

The second is the fund that invests solely in the short-term fully guaranteed obligations of the federal government, including both Treasury and federal agency issues. The third is the tax-exempt money market fund, which invests only in the short-term obligations of state and local issuers. The tax-exempt short-term fund offers no advantages to IRA owners, inevitably either paying less than comparable taxable issues, or paying well only because it is composed of rather risky obligations.

To the extent—and only to the extent—that money market mutual funds are invested in U.S. government obligations, they are government-guaranteed. Those money market funds that are composed wholly of such obligations are just as secure as federally insured bank deposits or CDs. However, they tend to pay a little less than other money market accounts because federal short-term obligations, being the most secure of all, generally pay less than any other debt obligations.

Those money market mutual funds that are not so composed and therefore guaranteed are not federally protected. Some are protected by private insurance, but *there is real question as to whether any private insurance arrangement would be strong enough to protect investors against the kinds of truly massive problems that would arise in a national or world financial crisis.* That kind of insurance might protect considerably, however, in the event of crisis in an individual fund, as from major mismanagement or fraud. None of this has been tested, though, at least as of this writing, for these funds have so far encountered neither general nor specific crises, and have an extraordinarily good safety record at a time when banks all over the country have been failing and many bank depositors not protected by federal insurance are consequently in great trouble.

On the other hand, many money market mutual funds invest in such highly questionable instruments as bank jumbo certificates of deposit, which are usually for sums much higher than the $100,000 deposit insurance limit, and therefore vulnerable to bank failure. So far, money market funds have been nimble enough to pull their funds out before disasters have happened, but there is no real guarantee that every set of money market fund managers will always be that agile.

Indeed, you can reasonably expect just the opposite. Sooner or later one or more money market funds will be caught in some banking collapse, to the detriment of their fund's shareholders. Note that Moody's has begun to monitor and rate bank CDs and other bank obligations. It is true that money market funds greatly diversify their holdings, so that a single bank failure, no matter how large, is unlikely to seriously affect the total worth of any fund. Serious impairment could happen in a general financial crisis, but only then.

As a practical matter, money market mutual funds operate much like variable rate short-term bank CDs. Generally, they are even shorter term than the bank CDs, usually making share value adjustments and compounding at least daily. Like bank IRAs, their opening and carrying costs are small to nonexistent. Many also offer such additional quasi-banking services as limited check-drawing privileges.

Their rates of interest vary with market conditions. Being invested in very short-term instruments, they respond more swiftly to those market conditions than do even the shortest term bank variable rate CDs, and certainly far more swiftly than any fixed rate CDs, which by their nature must pay interest reflecting market conditions and bank willingness to pay at the time the CD was bought. Therefore, in periods of rising interest rates, CD interest rates tend to lag behind the rates paid by more interest-sensitive money market funds.

Conversely, in periods of falling interest rates, money market rates tend to fall faster than bank CD rates, which reflect the higher-interest conditions prevailing when the CDs were bought. Note that these are only tendencies, though; competitive conditions may cause many large, well-established, federally insured banking institutions to offer short-term IRA interest rates a little higher than those available from money market mutual funds, even when interest rates are expected to rise.

When not used for IRAs, money market mutual funds are good for holding short-term savings; they are completely liquid and sometimes have effective rates higher than those offered by competing liquid money market accounts at banks, which often load on miscellaneous service charges that can appreciably lower the net effective yields actually paid. When used for IRAs, the same basic reasons are present for putting short-term money into such money market funds, to hold until higher yield investments are bought. But remember that there can be charges of $5 to $20 for moving money from one kind of IRA to another, as when you want to move money out of a money market mutual fund IRA into a mutual fund IRA or a self-directed IRA.

Also recall that some banks and other IRA trustees are reluctant to part with profitable IRA money in a timely way, which can operate to your disadvantage when you want to make such a move. When you want to buy into a mutual fund or a common stock, you are very likely to want to buy *now*, the day you make the decision. And that is the right way; the right timing is very often essential to the success of the move. An IRA trustee that holds your money for two weeks can destroy or seriously impair your investment opportunity, and that limits the usefulness of many bank accounts and money market mutual funds as short-term money storage devices for IRAs.

There is a way to use the device for IRAs rather painlessly, though. Many large financial organizations are actively promoting the one-stop financial supermarket approach to investing, in the process setting up a whole range of vehicles, techniques, and kinds of transactions under one roof. That is what you encounter today when you walk into such diverse organizations as Sears, Merrill Lynch, Prudential, Citibank, Chase, and the Bank of America. In those circumstances, it may be easy, quick, and inexpensive to move money from one IRA to another, just as it is easy to move IRA money between mutual funds in a "family" of related funds managed by one mutual funds organization. That can be a real advantage, for although no one has really yet developed a fully one-stop approach for IRA money, such partially effective one-stop approaches can make much easier the task of moving IRA money around to meet investment opportunities and satisfy your financial planning needs.

Stock Funds

The largest number of mutual funds are those investing in common stocks. These stock funds, or equity funds, are potentially the most confusing kinds of mutual funds for small investors, for the same fund may very well be described in both selling and analytical materials by two or more different kinds of descriptive names. For example, a fund organized to invest in the common stocks of small, highly volatile companies in the very new genetic engineering industry may variously be called an "aggressive growth" fund, a "maximum growth" fund, a "sector" fund, a "special interest" fund, and a "high risk" fund. All are correct, depending on who is selling, who is buying, and who is analyzing the fund and its underlying securities investments.

To begin to sort it out a bit, note that there are really three kinds of classification schemes in this area. The first describes the fund essentially by its possible rewards, the second by the degree of risk to its buyers, and the third by the mix of stocks the funds invest in.

Since small investors need to know most of all what potential risks and rewards are involved in the several kinds of possible investments, it seems appropriate here to describe stock or equity funds first in terms of risks and potential rewards and then to describe some special kinds of funds by their investments.

Aggressive Growth Funds

These are also called *maximum capital appreciation funds;* both phrases describe the aim of the fund's investment managers to grow the value of the common stocks in the fund as rapidly as possible, normally by investing in the fast-moving, highly speculative stocks of small companies.

These are the high-flying funds, the ones that grow very rapidly when the general level of the stock market is heading up; their successful top managers become media celebrities as long as things are going well. By the same token, they are also very properly described as "high-risk" funds, for that is exactly what they are. In the investment business, yesterday's celebrity may be today's forgotten investment manager, and yesterday's speculating, winning small investor is today's forgotten loser, never mentioned in advertising copy that extols the virtues of funds that have grown by hundreds of percent in only a few short years.

What goes up much faster than its surrounding markets must inevitably come down at least as fast. If the kinds of highly speculative stocks that aggressive growth, high-risk funds trade in were even somewhat safe, investment professionals all over the world would be buying them and bidding them up out of sight in the process. When all or almost all the stocks in a mutual fund portfolio are high-risk stocks, it makes little sense to speak of the benefits of diversification, for they are then nonexistent. It may be entirely valid to want to bet that a particular fund management will do well, and in essence to gamble on just that by purchasing fund shares, but it makes no sense at all to do that with any part of your vitally important, very long-term, highly tax-advantaged IRA money.

The same goes for some funds that call themselves only *sector* or *special interest* funds, about which more later. A fund that invests in the securities of a particular industry may be in both large and small companies in a relatively stable industry, and may have a moderate risk and a moderate chance of gain. But a fund invested wholly or mainly in small companies in a single industry may be even more risky than an aggressive growth fund invested in many kinds of stocks, for then it is not only general market fortunes that may help it grow or lose, but much narrower specific industry developments, as well.

The nub of the matter here is that high-flying funds must take high risks to get and keep up very high rates of fund value growth, and that high risks and IRA money should not mix, no matter how many get-rich-quick stories any of us hear or read.

Growth Funds

These are also high-risk, high-growth-potential common stock funds that are managed somewhat less adventurously than the very highly speculative aggressive growth funds. It is mostly a matter of degree; in either a sharply rising or a sharply falling stock market, both kinds of funds may advance, decline, and fluctuate a great deal. This kind of growth fund may invest in somewhat larger companies in industries thought to offer great growth possibilities, though stocks in those industries may have been bid up very high, and dividends are small to nonexistent.

A well-established no-load fund of this sort, with a good track record, may be a reasonable candidate for a small portion of your IRA money. That will especially be so for those who are relatively young, with decades of working time before them, or for those who at any age have quite substantial other investment assets developing.

Note, however, that tax advantage is already built into the potentially high growth stock or stock fund, in that you will pay no taxes on paper gains until they are realized through sale. For people with other investment assets, it may be best to use IRA funds to shield investment income that might otherwise be taxed, putting tax-advantaged long-term securities more into the rest of your investment portfolio.

Growth and Income Funds

These are common stock funds that aim to produce dividend income as well as growth. As a practical matter, this means investing mutual fund money in the relatively stable stocks of larger, well-established companies with good dividend payout records, as well as in somewhat more speculative stocks with high potential for growth but little or no dividend payouts to offer. These funds, by their nature, offer somewhat more safety and somewhat less growth than the more adventurous growth and aggressive growth funds, though in sharply down markets they may go down in share value almost as quickly.

When investing in such funds with taxable money, it is possible to take dividends, often in the form of monthly dividend checks, or to reinvest and compound dividends in place, in the fund. When investing with IRA money, all dividends are left in to compound, along with any gains realized on sale of fund shares.

Purchased on a no-load basis, these funds, with their somewhat greater stability, will in some periods of market upsurge and interest rate decline be good candidates for your IRA money. You will have to watch them rather carefully, though, as you watch all your investments, for you may want to shift out of them into other funds in a family of funds or into other kinds of investments as market conditions change.

Income Funds

These are rather conservatively managed combined stock and bond funds; in an earlier day they were for that reason called *balanced funds*. They tend to invest in a mix of high-quality bonds and high-quality stocks that pay dividends; generally they prefer safety and assured dividend payouts over possible share growth. Some of the largest funds in the country continue to be balanced in this way, and do quite well; their managers move freely between stocks and bonds as market conditions indicate.

In some periods, the net dividends-plus-growth yield of these funds, compounding in place in IRAs, can greatly exceed the returns available from CDs and money market funds. For most of what should be conservatively managed

IRA money, these conservatively managed funds, bought on a no-load basis, seem the best mutual funds of all. Should personal financial plans and market conditions make a partial IRA move into mutual funds attractive, by all means seek out such balanced, or income, funds.

Sector or Special Interest Funds

In American marketing, the dominant approach continues to be "give the cats what they want to eat." On that theory, investment sellers have for the past quarter-century been creating mutual funds tailored to appeal to the popular investing tastes of the day.

In the 1960s, the last time mutual funds were in great vogue, investment sellers began to create many kinds of special purpose funds, organized to trade in stocks and debt obligations in groups of industries, single industries, and even in companies based on single commodities, such as gold. By the end of the 1960s, whatever was popular among investors—usually described as "hot"—was usually also available in mutual fund form. And because they were hot, they did well, as their underlying securities were bid up by speculators in booming markets.

But what is hot sooner or later becomes cold, and in the not-so-booming 1970s investors in hot, narrowly based special purpose or special interest funds suffered huge losses. Many of the funds went out of business or continue to exist only as shadows of their former selves. The large balanced funds did much, much better in down markets; many of them survived well and are growing again today. But the narrow funds did so badly that even the form fell out of favor for years.

In today's somewhat revived stock markets, special interest funds are back, usually now called *sector funds*. The new name for them is merely seller's art; they are the same old narrowly based securities funds, with the same old get-rich-quick appeal and the same old high risks.

The problem here is twofold. First, special interest funds

by their nature lose one of the key advantages of mutual funds: diversification. Many are so narrow, and composed of such speculative securities, that all or almost all their stocks are affected by the same kinds of favorable and unfavorable news and trends. If you are in a special interest oil and gas fund, and the price of oil goes down sharply, you are probably no better off than if you had bought only one or two of the stocks in the group, for all will go down together. Actually, you would probably be better off in that kind of situation to have your money in the two or three strongest companies in the group, which may be better able to withstand adversity than the weaker companies.

Second, and related, such funds may be hard hit by specific events, even when general market levels are rising. In that respect, they are even worse speculations than the most speculative broadly based aggressive growth funds.

These special interest funds are not really suitable for IRAs, no matter how good their recent track records look and how well investment sellers speak of this one or that.

International Funds

The financial marketplace of the 1980s is also an increasingly close-knit international financial marketplace. Investment professionals today can and often do trade twenty-four hours a day and seven days a week, through a fully computerized worldwide network of financial people and institutions. They trade in stocks, public and private debt obligations, commodity and financial instrument futures, Eurodollars, and a good deal more, for the number and variety of available trading vehicles and techniques increase around the world just as quickly as they do in the United States.

In the international marketplace, however, there are a great many more uncertainties and risks than there are in the United States, and it is at the same time far more difficult to stay informed than it is in the United States. IRA owners who might want to buy the stock of even the best known and most stable of foreign companies are best advised to do so through international mutual funds, rather than on their own. That is so even when the company you are interested in is listed on a large U.S. stock exchange and widely traded here. For small investors, it is just too difficult to keep up properly with all the main factors that can affect the performance and prospects of a company headquartered abroad. Here, and here alone, it may even make sense to pay front or back loads if you strongly want to invest abroad, for you will find that the number of excellently and conservatively managed mutual funds in this area is small.

Generally, *international mutual funds* are those investing solely in shares and debt obligations originating abroad. Funds called *global* usually also invest in U.S.-originated shares and obligations, although their main emphasis is international. However they are named, their main function is to act as pools of professionally managed internationally invested money, moving from vehicle to vehicle and area to area as market conditions indicate. Some are worldwide funds, while others focus on specific geographic areas, such as the Pacific basin.

You can reasonably expect a proliferation of international funds in this period. As strong, competitive foreign economies rise—notably that of Japan—American investment professionals seek opportunities abroad. And as the computerized international nonstop trading network grows, it becomes easier and easier to seek such opportunities. At this writing, half a dozen new international funds have been recently organized, and by the time you read this page there may be many more, with new and old funds alike competing for the investment dollars of Americans increasingly interested in investing abroad.

Note, though, that as in any new, popular investment area, there will be "hot" funds, organized to make speculative killings and to attract large numbers of small investors entranced by very recent hot track records. Note also that out in the rest of the world the opportunities for fraud are much greater than in the United States, for securities regulation in many countries is far less stringent than in this country. Note further that aside from fraud, the risks out there are more diverse than those encountered here. All that together is a prescription for the development of some very attractive-looking speculative funds indeed, which go up and up—until they come down, down, and down, often accompanied by great scandals. That is what happened when the Cornfeld international mutual funds empire collapsed in the 1960s, and a very sober look at the burgeoning international securities and mutual funds market indicates that such possibilities will soon exist again.

On the other hand, international mutual funds may quite legitimately prove very attractive in some periods, as when companies based in other nations are profiting handsomely from the adverse American balance of trade and their own favorable production costs. Should you want to go in that direction with some of your IRA money, though, be quite sure to do it in successfully and conservatively managed funds with good track records, rather than with unproven international funds. There are a few good, seasoned international funds; it is those that are worth looking at.

Funds of Funds

Mention of the long-gone Cornfeld empire conjures up memories of the investment vehicle known as the *fund of funds*. This is simply a mutual fund organized to invest in the shares of other mutual funds, most notably in a single family of funds. The device seems to be reviving, in a small way, which makes it worth some brief comments.

Funds of funds are wonderful—for their promoters, not their investors. They provide a magnificent opportunity for collecting two layers of fees from the same investment dollars. Indeed, the only really good way to collect two sets of investment management fees is to sell a share, charge for its management, buy it for a fund of funds, and charge for management again.

Actually, this double-charging technique is not likely to achieve wide use again, as regulators and substantial numbers of investors remember the 1960s at least well enough to be wary of funds of funds. In addition, there are ways of charging now that were not widely used in the 1960s, such as the back load and the yearly distribution fee on top of investment management fees. Should anyone try to sell you shares in a fund of funds, back away fast.

Municipal Bond Funds

Like the municipal bonds of which they are composed, the main attraction of municipal bond funds is that they are tax-advantaged. That tax advantage has no significance at all for IRA owners, for IRAs are already tax-advantaged. That is why municipals and municipal bond funds must be evaluated as comparative investment opportunities by IRA owners without reference to tax advantage, but only compared with other investments as to straightforward risk and yield.

Seen that way, *municipal bond funds are clearly unsuitable for IRAs, no matter how hard they are sold as good IRA investments*. They are not. What is mildly astonishing is that some people do buy them for their IRAs, even though their risks are large and their rewards are slim compared with other investments of the same quality. As previously discussed, very many municipals are intrinsically high-risk investments, because of the instability of their state and local issuers; their private insurance does not eliminate the high risk. In this area, it is wise to take rating service classifications with a grain of salt, for big, intrinsically risky municipal issues may carry private insurance that will not be able or willing to cover if there is a major default.

Therefore the municipal or municipal mutual fund that pays as much as, or even a little more than, fully guaranteed long-term federal debt issues is in no way comparable. For IRAs, without the municipal bond tax advantage in the picture, the federally guaranteed issue is a far better invest-ment. It may become a close question for some investors working with fully taxable money, for a 10% municipal bond return can mean a 20% real after-tax yield. But there is no question for IRA owners at all, for the safe federal issue yielding as much or almost as much is a much better invest-ment than the high-risk municipal or municipal bond fund.

There is another risk, as well, stemming from the tax politics of the time. Should municipals at any time lose all or a significant part of their tax advantage because of tax law changes, municipals issuers will have to generate new bonds that pay much higher rates of interest than current bonds, for that will be the only way to attract bond buyers. Then the existing high risks will be magnified, as municipals issuers are forced to take on much larger interest obligations. In those circumstances, previously issued municipals and the funds holding them will lose much of their market value, and unfortunate bond and fund owners will be faced with choos-ing between selling out at large losses or holding on to increasingly risky issues at too-low rates of return.

Given the current risks, the possible addition of greater risks, and their low rates of return without tax advantage, municipal bond funds should not be seen as proper invest-ments for IRAs.

Ginnie Mae and Other Government Plus Funds

In the mid-1980s, one of the fastest-growing sections of the mutual fund industry has been the *Ginnie Mae fund*, sometimes called the *Government Plus fund*. These funds have been enormously attractive to risk-averse investors, who buy them because they believe the funds offer a combination of federal guarantees, relatively high payouts, and even some state and local tax avoidance. IRA owners do not benefit from any such tax advantages, as IRAs are already far better tax-advantaged, but they have still bought large quantities of these funds for their combination of safety and yield.

The basic mechanism involved in the creation of such a fund is the purchase and repackaging of large-denomination debt obligations, and the sale of shares in the investment pool so created. This is not essentially different from what happens when a money market fund buys large-denomination short-term obligations, or a unit trust sells pieces of a specified pool of bonds. Indeed, those are the two kinds of funds created with Ginnie Maes and other federal obligations. Some Ginnie Mae funds are mutual funds, selling shares in a constantly changing body of investments, as fund managers invest and reinvest the money in the fund. Others are unit trusts, created with specific federal debt obligations repackaged in smaller units for ease of sale.

The resulting funds have advertised themselves as fully federally insured, for the Ginnie Maes wholly or largely underlying them are federally insured. They have also advertised—and produced—yields considerably higher than those available from shorter-term money market funds and CDs; some of them have produced yields one, even two or three points higher than the longer-term CDs and long-term federal bonds. They have been particularly attractive during periods of lowering interest rates, for then large numbers of the mortgages underlying the Ginnie Maes in the fund investment pools are high-interest mortgages that have not yet been renegotiated by homeowners.

Ginnie Mae and Government Plus funds have paid relatively good rates of return in the mid-1980s, and to some degree are as safe as their sellers claim they are, making them reasonably good candidates for IRA investments. At the same time, it should be pointed out that *much of their success in the financial marketplace is because they are wonderful sources of income for sellers*. They are sold hard, and both advertisements and face-to-face sellers often very badly mislead prospective buyers, for they are not quite as safe as they seem, either as to yield or federal guarantees. Most of them do pay substantial front-load commissions to their sellers, though, and some pay commissions every year, as an alternative to, or on top of, those front-load commissions.

The federal government guarantees the interest and repayment of principal promises of its own debt obligations, including Ginnie Maes and other federal issues in the mutual fund or unit trust investment pools. It does not insure against fluctuations in debt obligation market prices, as when interest rates go up and bond prices go down to adjust rates of return to current market levels. That is the standard bond market risk, and is in no way changed by the federal interest and principal repayment guarantees.

People investing in these kinds of funds may, however be taking considerably greater risks than market fluctuation— not enough to destroy the investment, given the federal guarantees, but certainly enough to put quite a dent in it in some circumstances. For to build up their yields in a highly competitive fund marketplace, most of these funds also invest some portion of fund assets in highly speculative repurchase agreements (repos) and in futures, as well as in somewhat less speculative but still risky covered call options.

That is understandable, in competitive terms, for it is the only way to build Ginnie Mae and other government yields up appreciably above long-term Treasury bond yields. Ginnie Maes by themselves can be counted on to yield $1/2\%$ to 1% more than long-term Treasury bonds, depending upon the circumstances of the time, and other federal bond fund investments yield no better in the long run. That is scarcely enough to attract and hold investors, for it would then soon become obvious that, once investment management and sales charges were taken into account, the funds would actually yield less than direct purchase of the bonds themselves. Aside from that, it takes only a few adventurous fund managements seeking competitive advantage in a battle for investment dollars to push all or almost all Ginnie Mae and Government Plus managements into such speculative practices.

On the other hand, it can be relatively expensive to buy

government bonds directly. They are sold through dealers, and there are charges of $25 to $45 per transaction. There can also be excess profit-taking by dealers on sales of small quantities of bonds, with selling prices slightly higher and buying prices slightly lower than those commanded by large institutional bond traders. This, too, is understandable, for such small transactions are more bother and cost to dealers than profit; but the net effect is extra cost to small bond investors.

If you mean to be a thoroughly active IRA owner, it can make sense to buy and sell bonds through a self-directed IRA, rather than setting up a Ginnie Mae or Government Plus fund account, and to handle dividends by sweeping them into a short-term money market account, either in a bank or in a money market mutual fund. If, though, you do not wish to watch and manage quite that closely, and want to put some of your IRA money into long-term government debt obligations, it may make sense to buy shares in this kind of mutual fund, with automatic dividend reinvestment.

Should you decide to buy shares in this kind of fund, by all means seek out a true no-load fund, even though there may not be very many in this area. There is even less reason here than in equity funds to pay high selling fees, for all the underlying securities here pay in the same narrow range; any significantly larger payouts exist only because significantly larger risks are being taken by some mutual fund managements.

When assessing these kinds of funds, it is also wise to bear in mind that promised rates of return may, to some extent, disappear right before your eyes. Homeowners renegotiate loans when interest rates go down appreciably; Ginnie Maes are based upon existing mortgages. When those mortgages are replaced by new lower-interest mortgages, the Ginnie Maes built from them are paid off early, and disappear. When you hold a unit trust, that means early repayment of principal. When you hold fund shares, that means replacement of high interest Ginnie Maes with lower-interest Ginnie Maes, and lower rates of payout to shareholders.

Ginnie Maes are in this respect most emphatically not like long- or medium-term federal debt obligations, and the 12-year to 14-year average duration ascribed to Ginnie Maes by many investment sellers has nothing to do with current mortgage market realities. Therefore also note that the seller who urges you to buy a front-loaded fund because you will be spreading the load over many years of ownership may be seriously misleading you, either knowingly or because the seller simply has not thought out the real nature of the investment.

The next section of this work consists of nine sample IRA planning situations, to illustrate how you might go about applying the advice contained in this book in your own specific financial planning. It is followed by a glossary of key financial terms.

Nine IRA Planning Situations

Here are some rather diverse examples of how the analysis and advice offered in this book might work out in practice. The people and specifics of each situation are constructed for purpose of illustration, though these are precisely the kinds of situations encountered in the real world. All the names used are entirely fictitious, and any resemblance to living persons is entirely accidental.

Note that all the examples here are set within the contexts provided by individual goals and full lifetime financial plans. IRA funds do not exist in a vacuum; what you do with them depends upon how well you seek and handle the whole financial side of life.

Note also that these examples contain recommendations that may change a great deal as general economic and financial market conditions change. For example, early in 1986, when these examples are being prepared, it seems appropriate to recommend some movement of IRA funds into stocks and selected stock-based mutual funds. By the time you read these pages, the financial marketplace situation may very well call for either a strong move away from stocks in a sharply declining stock market, or a much greater move into stocks, should a long-term, prosperity-based bull market develop. These examples illustrate, far more than they recommend courses of action. These illustrative examples assume that the 1986 tax law has no impact upon these situations. All the people either have incomes low enough for them to qualify for full contribution deductibility, or are self-employed, with no other pension plans.

1. Jim Grey and Mary Wells Grey

They had not realized it would come to so much, and getting it properly invested was turning out to be something of a chore for people who had never before paid much attention to investments.

There really hadn't been much point, as there was never very much to invest. Jim, at 50, had been working for the same company for just under 20 years, and Mary had been at home with the children. Starting as a field sales representative, he had gradually worked his way up to a pretty good marketing management job, carrying a reasonably good salary and some excellent benefits, but they had never managed to save much out of his salary. That wasn't a matter of high living; their reasons were named Kathy, Joe, and Darlene, and anyone who has tried to put three children through college at once knows why Jim and Mary Grey had very little cash left over after paying their monthly bills.

What they had was the house, which had gained a lot of value in the last 20 years, and a good company pension plan, which with Social Security was going to give them enough to get by on in their later years—after they got the college debts paid off. Beyond that, there was some life insurance, a small quantity of stock in Jim's company, and a little cash for current needs.

It was because of the college costs, really, that Jim made the big decision to take the new job offered by one of his company's smaller competitors. The job was less secure, but it had more responsibility and a bigger salary. Besides, he reasoned, nothing was all that secure in these times; there had been some merger talk after his big, stable company had experienced a couple of sub-par years.

Jim's pension plan payout came to a little over $200,000. A lot of money; more than Jim and Mary had ever expected to see. And a lot of taxable money, too; that's why he rolled the whole thing over into a tax-advantaged IRA fund and set about building that fund as a portable personal pension plan. Ultimately, Jim actually wound up with several IRAs, developed out of that big lump sum pension payout, though he thinks of it as one IRA fund. He and Mary have also opened other IRAs, contributing their maximum $2,000 each yearly, because Mary is now working, too; but these additional IRAs are separate from the rolled-over pension plan payout.

The main early problem was that Jim and Mary did not know how to invest the money, for they had never before done anything like this or handled anything like the sums of money involved. Knowing that they needed help, they did what so many other astute people have done before them; they asked around, querying their friends, talking with their accountant and lawyer, answering advertisements to secure sales literature, and then fielding and learning from the resulting inevitable flood of selling telephone calls.

Eventually, their accountant led them to a financial adviser she had been working with for years, after first very carefully telling them that if they did commission-generating financial business with the adviser, the adviser would be splitting some of the early resulting commissions with the accountant. That was reassuring. Jim and Mary had no concern about the commission splitting in principle, but would have had great reservations if it had not been disclosed up front.

Jim and Mary respected their accountant, and respected the financial adviser to whom they were introduced, who turned out to be a thoroughly experienced certified financial planner. Even so, they asked the adviser the whole searching list of questions contained earlier in this book, adding a few of their own. Satisfied with the answers, with their accountant's recommendation, and with the two planning meetings held with the adviser, they were ready to pay a $250 consulting fee and to take some of the adviser's financial planning recommendations, which were not limited to the kind of investment advice they had originally come seeking.

Before even discussing investments, but after seeing their whole financial situation, their adviser suggested that they buy some additional term life insurance; with two children still in college and Jim's company-paid life insurance dropping off, they were underinsured. There will be company-paid life insurance at Jim's new company, but they are ignoring that, after finding out that his previous company's life insurance could be converted to individual life insurance only at prohibitively high costs. Actually, Jim had always been somewhat underinsured, with the gap between what he had and what his survivors might need growing wider as inflation sapped the value of the dollar over the years.

They decided to buy the additional term life insurance the adviser recommended, and through the adviser. That resulted in some modest commissions, and that was all right with Jim and Mary. The advice was sound, and the insurance rates they paid were competitive; they checked on that.

On the investment side, Jim and Mary had been rather concerned about rolling the whole pension payout over into an IRA fund, reasoning that if anything went wrong with Jim's new job they might have to tap the IRA funds—and pay high penalties—to make ends meet. But after thinking it through, they realized that the penalties would be far outweighed by the tax-free accumulation that would occur in even a few years. They did, however, decide to keep most of their IRA money quite liquid, as they might need to turn it into cash. They also decided to avoid all the front-load and back-load charges that might lock them into investments they might want to turn into cash, and to avoid potential interest penalties on early CD withdrawals, as well.

They also decided to buy into a family of no-load mutual

funds, for this was a period in which the stock market was rising strongly, and they felt after investigation that it was likely to continue to rise. Initially, they put most of that money into a large balanced fund with a good long-term track record, and smaller amounts into a somewhat more aggressively managed stock dividends and growth fund, a Ginnie Mae fund, and a smallish reserve in a money market mutual fund.

They will watch these funds very closely, moving their money without penalty of any sort from fund to fund as market conditions indicate. They had insisted that the investment adviser recommend such a no-load family of funds, rejecting two earlier recommendations, both of which were front-loaded. Indeed, they had been somewhat dismayed by those loaded fund recommendations, for they thought they might very well stem from the higher commissions paid by load funds. However, they were content to transact this part of their business through the adviser, on a no-load fund basis.

They also put a substantial chunk of their money into one- and two-year federally guaranteed CDs, feeling that they wanted the security of that federal guarantee and were willing to accept a lower return for it. They avoided the higher-paying longer-term CD's though. They reasoned that for higher returns they would go elsewhere, without having to run the risk of premature withdrawal interest penalties should they have to tap their IRA fund for current needs, or want to move some of their money for greater advantage within their IRAs.

The Ginnie Mae portion of their family of funds also reaches for that federal guarantee, as the Ginnie Maes comprising most of the fund are true federal agency debt obligations. The Ginnie Mae fund currently pays just as well as the longer-term CDs, is fully federally insured, and can be sold without penalty at any time. Even if there is some loss in the value of Ginnie Mae fund shares when they might need to sell them, that loss is likely to be far smaller than the large interest penalties they might have to pay on premature withdrawal of long-term CDs.

Jim and Mary had also thought about opening a self-directed brokerage account, for there are some investment moves they believe they may be able to make better and less expensively on their own. But they will defer that move, rightly thinking that they first have much to learn about investing. They will be doing that, later on, but with a discount broker, rather than through a higher-priced firm recommended by their investment adviser.

Jim and Mary rejected the suggestion that they buy single-premium deferred annuities with part of their IRA fund. This was a close question, for the current interest guarantees were attractive. But the annuities carried a back-load charge of 7%, going down 1% a year until there were no charges for selling after seven years of ownership. They did not want to lock themselves in that way.

They plan to reevaluate their holdings regularly, and at least once a year quite fully and formally with their account-ant and financial adviser. They recognize that nothing stands still, that no investments can be tucked away and forgotten, and that this kind of long-term game goes to those who are vigilant and increasingly skillful.

2. Sue Jones Weiss and Will Weiss

Sue and Will are doing pretty well; certainly a lot better than many of their friends. Since the farm equipment factory that was their Illinois town's biggest employer closed down two years ago, unemployment has become too much of a way of life for too many. But there are new signs of life and new employers now. The town will certainly survive, though some will go back to work for much less pay than before.

Sue will keep her job as a grade-school teacher, and Will will continue to bring in varying amounts of money as a freelance artist and photographer. Actually, Will is doing better than ever before; he is beginning to go up to Chicago for freelance advertising work quite regularly now. They need the additional money, too; they are both now in their mid-30s, and their two children, Ann and Carla, are beginning to grow up, need more things, and look forward to college in not so many years.

For the past five years, they have put most of their spare money into the house, in the process making it a far better place to live and simultaneously a far more valuable asset. Beyond that, what they have is a little stock left by Will's father, and the money in their IRAs, which they have been putting in for the past four years. It hasn't always been as much as they would have liked, but their joint IRA funds now total almost $14,000, to them a surprisingly large amount.

From the start, they have been thoroughly risk-averse, and have taken great care to put their money into short- and medium-term fully federally insured CDs. With all the bank failures, farm foreclosures, and factory closings that have plagued their part of the country, they have not been about to jeopardize even the smallest part of their IRA savings by putting their money into banks that pay a little more but are not federally insured; or into money market funds, no matter how safe they seemed. They have certainly not been willing to go into the stock market or other even more speculative investments, no matter how strong the market seemed.

But times, fears, and opportunities change. This year, as they do their annual review of the financial side of their lives, they find that CD rates have gone far down, while eager financial sellers and even some of their friends boast about the killings they are making in a surging stock market. Some of their friends have even gone in such clearly speculative directions as commodity and financial futures trading. No, they will not speculate with their long-term IRA money, but it makes them think about whether or not they may be missing some real opportunities through excess conservatism.

Their holdings and prospects are a little small for most professional financial advisers. They did buy a couple of books to carefully read, though, and then both attended a very good financial planning class at a local college. That, helped enormously when they sat down to have a serious planning discussion with their accountant. It all took a good deal of time, and it was worth it, for it laid the basis for a sound approach to lifetime financial planning, of which what to do with their IRA money is only a small part.

What they did with their IRA money was not to change direction, but to adjust focus a little. Still wanting the federal guarantees and unwilling to risk much on stock or bond market fluctuations, they left one-third of their money in one- and two-year federally guaranteed CDs, put one-third into a no-load Ginnie Mae fund that was part of a family of no-load funds, and put one-third into a balanced stock and bond mutual fund in the same family of funds.

They will get the safety they want in the CDs, with no possible direct loss of that part of their capital. They will run some risk with the Ginnie Mae fund if bond market conditions force fund share prices down, but little risk as to underlying interest and principal repayment promises, because of the federal guarantees. They will run risk with the money in the balanced fund, but will watch that investment very closely, and may do very well if the stock market continues to move strongly upward. They can also reasonably expect the professionals managing the balanced fund to move rather quickly away from stock shares, and into debt obligations and cash instruments, should the market begin to decline sharply.

3. Jane Reilly

Jane has been unemployed for seven months, and if she doesn't get a job by the end of the month she's going to have to tap her IRA for the rent. The unemployment compensation just isn't enough, and she has gone through her other savings, even though she has been living very carefully indeed.

Actually, she had thought all along that if the time came she would be able to borrow money against her IRA, and not have to touch it or pay penalty taxes on money withdrawn, just as if it were a passbook savings account. Not so. As soon as she raised the question at the bank that was holding her IRA-account CDs, she was told that the law precluded using IRA funds as collateral for a loan. Nor would the bank give her a personal loan on her signature, for without a job or other collateral she was viewed as a poor loan risk, even though her previous credit rating had been excellent.

So she will tap her IRA, by not rolling over a CD that is about to mature; that way she will avoid interest rate penalties for early withdrawal, although there will be unavoidable tax penalties on the IRA fund withdrawals made. She never wanted to do that, and it comes hard. On the other hand, she does have $12,000 in her IRA, and thinks that there is a very good chance that she never would have saved even a substantial fraction of that much without the savings incentives provided by the tax-free accumulation available in the IRA. As it has turned out, without that IRA money she would really be up against it.

As to the tax penalty, the money has accumulated tax-free for some years now, and she figures that even with the 10% penalty she is still way ahead of the game. In an ordinary, fully taxable bank account, without either tax-free accumulation or a tax penalty for early withdrawals, she would have netted much less than she will have after the penalty is paid. Nor is she drawing out all her IRA fund; she is quite likely to make it through with only a few thousand dollars of her IRA money, with the rest continuing to accumulate tax-free.

4. Jane Ward Dodds and Sam Dodds

To understand their concerns, you have to know that Jane and Sam are both Depression kids. Not recession— depression; the Great Depression. Both in their 50s now, they very well remember growing up on a little pork, a lot of beans, and clothes that looked like one big patch.

They are savers; in the jargon of the financial trade, risk-averse savers, people who will sacrifice reward in favor of safety every day of the week. They both work at good civil service jobs, make considerably more than they spend, and have among other things amassed IRAs worth almost $20,000, all invested in fully federally guaranteed CDs.

They are worried about the worth of the federal guarantee. With the huge federal deficits, immense and obviously bad foreign loans, bank closures, farm failures, corporate bankruptcies, and all the rest, they have been seriously thinking about doing what they did in the mid-1970s: move into gold, gems, collectibles, guns, and grub—the kinds of hard goods stores of value that were thought to be the best ways to beat inflation and perhaps even to survive economic collapse. At this point, they don't know whether they want to put any more money into federally guaranteed IRA funds, or whether it may even be time to pull their money out of IRAs altogether, paying the tax penalties.

The answer, if there really is an answer to these entirely understandable concerns, is that the United States and its government's financial guarantees are about as good as you are going to get. That is why investment money continues to flow into the United States from all over the world. Not "hot" money, which follows interest rates; but investment money, the kind of money that goes into real estate and company ownership. Short of a complete change of social system, the U.S. government should be relied upon to pay up on its direct payment promises, for example federal deposit insurance guarantees.

5. Tom Martin

Tom is having a ball with his IRA. He's moving his money around, taking advantage of all kinds of new opportunities in a surging market that looks as if it's going right through the roof, and doesn't have to worry about the tax implications of his many and varied trades at all, which is the beauty of the IRA for a real stock trader like Tom.

Four years ago, when he started his IRA, he was very conservative; far too conservative, as he now sees it. All he managed to do in those four years was to build up a total fund of a little under $10,000, investing the money in such very safe, dull things as CDs, Ginnie Mae funds, and later balanced mutual funds. But the way even the conservative balanced funds did in a surging market, coupled with a good talk he had with a financial consultant working for a major securities firm, really opened his eyes.

He had met the financial consultant at a party. The next day he opened a self-directed trading account with him, and it has been all up from then on. In the first year, piling killing trade on killing trade, mostly in the stocks of young, vital, growing companies, he almost doubled his money. And those are companies with nowhere to go but up, in a market that's headed for the stratosphere.

What Tom has found particularly impressive is that his broker, the very same financial consultant he met at the party, is so willing to put in so much time and effort on his behalf, bringing new companies to his attention and calling him when the time is right for trades. Tom couldn't possibly have done it on his own. Yes, of course, his broker is making money on the transactions, but how much can a broker make on a little guy like Tom? This is the case of a broker going far beyond the call of duty, and doing a great deal more than he needs to, for a friend.

Yep, there is one born every minute. Tom's case is perhaps somewhat overstated, for purposes of emphasis. But not by much. A whole new generation of innocents is being led to slaughter in rising markets in these years, and all too often by investment professionals who should know better. And often do.

There is unethical and sometimes illegal churning of

accounts throughout the financial marketplace, and the cumulative commissions resulting from the churning of even small accounts—if there are enough of them—can add to some brokerage incomes quite considerably. Tom is paying for scores of full commission, highly speculative trades, when he should be paying for a much smaller number of sound trades; that is quite aside from the question of whether he should be using a discount broker, rather than a full-commission broker.

Even more disastrously, Tom is being led up the garden path, for what goes up must come down, as stock markets have proved as long as they have existed. Ultimately, if he does not reverse course, Tom will lose his shirt speculating, and his losses will be accelerated by the costs of those expensive multiple trades. Worst of all, he is doing it with his IRA money, which could grow so well and safely because of its tax advantage, if he will only develop the wit to invest it conservatively once again.

6. Bryan Smith and Sally Kaplan Smith

Sally and Bryan want to use their IRA money to swing a little free, in a very modest way. They are doing quite well financially; have good jobs in middle management, excellent profit-sharing and pension plans, a home, and some other securities; and see no reason not to use their IRA funds as a trading fund. They don't see themselves as either speculators or investment professionals, but they are quite willing to take some modest risks.

To them, that does not mean taking all their IRA money into a fast-moving self-directed brokerage account. Far from it; they are both smart enough to recoil from the kind of broker who wants to take them in and out of speculative investments. They have instead opened a self-directed account with a discount broker, arranging to sweep free cash into a money market fund as it becomes available in the self-directed account. They are relying upon their own reading and constant discussion and analysis of the limited number of stocks and bonds they follow for their trading moves, and are doing quite well on that basis.

They also follow wider trends, and are moving some of their IRA money around in a family of no-load funds in accordance with their views of the main trends at work. For example, they will move some funds into high-risk, extremely aggressive growth funds that are doing extremely well when market conditions and the investment skills of fund managers converge—and then move that money to far more conservatively managed funds and sometimes into money market funds when market conditions seem to be changing for the worse. Should market and general economic conditions change greatly for the worse, they will consider moving their money out of stocks altogether, and into such vehicles as federally insured CDs and federal bonds.

7. George Walters

In December, George did his annual financial evaluation. The house had appreciated a good deal more, though of course he had no plans to sell it. Single parents with two teenagers doing well in an excellent school system don't sell houses so fast. His modest securities portfolio had also done well, both the taxable part and the considerably larger IRA portion. He was very pleased about that; last year's decision to move most of his IRA money out of CDs and into a self-directed brokerage account was paying off, even though brokerage fees were quite high. The net of all the securities transactions was a much more valuable IRA fund than he would have had if the money had been left in CDs.

George did his preliminary tax workup, saw that it was possible to put $2,000 more in the coming year into his IRA and did so in January, putting the money into his self-directed IRA brokerage account and buying 500 shares of a very promising new issue at $2, along with $1,000 more in zero-coupon bonds, for balancing purposes.

Late in January, his youngest, Jimmy, came down with a

king-sized case of the flu, and infected Annie, George, and probably half the neighborhood besides. They were all sick for weeks, and George had to postpone his business travel plans. Then, in late February, he finally did take off for almost three weeks on the road, returning to a whole series of minor but necessarily absorbing business and personal problems.

When he came up for air in the middle of April, George realized that the economic stories he had been vaguely scanning in the newspaper all during the period added up to a major change in investment climate, and that he had best look to his investments before it was too late.

But it was; what had gone up had come down, as these things always must. It was, in sum, simple enough. For a whole host of rather complicated national and international reasons, interest rates had gone up and stayed up. As a direct result, stock prices had gone down, staying down, and were still dropping. The most speculative of the stocks, which had gone up most, came down catastrophically, which certainly included Walter's nice little new issue at $2, now selling for $0.70 a share, along with some other high flyers he had bought last year.

Nor was that all of it. The zero-coupon bonds had been sold to him as a matter of balancing somewhat "aggressive," meaning speculative, investments with sure, safe bond investments. They were said to be ideal for IRAs, for the tax-advantage in the IRA fund made it possible to own zeroes without having to pay taxes on imputed interest every year. However, when interest rates went up, down came the value of zero-coupon bonds paying previous lower rates of interest, which were far more volatile without the moderating influence of the interest payments, which had been stripped away to create zeroes. The payment promises were still there; and since these were Treasury issues, the paymnent promise was entirely sound. But the bonds themselves were worth much less than before on the open market, and George was faced with the alternative of selling them at a loss to free his money for higher-yielding investments, or holding on in hope that interest rates would go down again, restoring the market value of his bonds.

What he did was to sell some of his stocks, holding some in hope of future appreciation, and to hold most of his zeroes, reasoning that interest rates would come down again and that the payment promises were good. He has stayed partly in a self-directed IRA account, though, reasoning that his error was in speculating too much and watching too little, rather than in moving out of his CDs.

With interest rates up, he has moved some of his money back into CDs, and is watching interest rates and market trends very closely, so that he can move into less speculative stocks and bonds as conditions permit.

8. Ann Williams Rivers and Gary Rivers

This year, after they both received excellent raises and a great deal of other encouragement on their jobs, Ann and Gary began to look at their IRA money a little differently. Until now, they had seen the IRA money as a long-term savings fund, aimed at helping them through their later years if they needed it, and also as a kind of ultimate last resort source of cash if things went very bad and they needed to get some money, whatever the costs and tax penalties.

But now, both only in their early 30s, with good jobs, company pension plans, and some savings besides, they are thinking about swinging a lot more free, by putting their IRA money into the kinds of high-flying stocks and mutual funds their friends are recommending. One of their friends has introduced them to her broker, who is about their age and a wonderful woman. They are assured that in these markets it is possible to double your money in a year or two, especially if you don't have to worry about the tax implications of some very lucrative kinds of short-term trades.

And yet Ann and Gary are not entirely innocents, as so many of their friends seem to them to be. They know about get-rich-quick stock speculation from close up; Ann's father never tires of telling them that he lost enough at the end of the 1960s to have put her through college twice. Their situation has changed, though; that is real, and they both recognize that changed personal circumstances should rightly cause them to reevaluate investment goals and strategies.

Their response is to change the composition of their IRA investment fund, but not radically. They have been mostly in CDs; now, with lower interest rates and better opportunities elsewhere, they will move some of that money into a no-load family of funds, first into a Ginnie Mae fund and a balanced fund.

Next year, or the year after, they may open up a self-directed brokerage account, not because they intend to use it for speculation, but rather because they think that, in the long run, they should learn how to make their own right invest-ment moves, and a self-directed IRA can be a wonderful self-educating vehicle.

9. Harriet Wilson

When the IRA fund got up to $10,000, Harriet knew that it was time—perhaps a little past time—to consult a financial adviser. She didn't exactly have an accountant or attorney to ask for a referral, since her tax return was done by a tax preparation service, so she asked around among her friends. She came up with a financial consultant employed by a very large stock brokerage firm, who came warmly recommended by two friends who had been making money with him, one for two years and one for a little over one year. She called, made an appointment, loaded her last two tax returns and some other information into her briefcase, and went to see him in his very attractive office. Nice building, nice decorations, a lot of activity, and obviously money being made all around her.

It went well at first. Joseph had a lot of very perceptive questions, carefully took down her answers, and from the start went far beyond the IRA fund, and into the big, important lifetime financial planning questions. Actually, she felt that an account as small as hers scarcely justified the attention; he was charging her nothing for the initial consultation, and the commissions she could generate would scarcely pay him for the time he had already put in.

But then it started to go not quite so well. Harriet is pretty good at selling; you have to be to make it as an interior decorator these days. Perhaps even more to the point, she thinks she knows when she is being sold, rather than counseled, and after about half an hour she began to think that was beginning to happen. It was. What eventually emerged was a rather hard sell of a heavily front-loaded family of mutual funds.

Ultimately, with promises to seriously consider everything he had said, and much thanks for all the time he had given her, she ran, which was precisely the right thing to do. When a financial adviser tries to sell you on first interview, you run, and you do not return. Harriet was not particularly daunted by the experience, though; that sort of thing is part of the game, and you cannot expect to find the right financial adviser on first try, no matter how well recommended that adviser comes. She will try again, more than once if necessary, and will come up with someone she can work with; there are many ethical, skilled financial advisers out there.

Glossary

In every unfamiliar field, learning the language is half the battle. In this instance, it is the language of finance and investment that needs to be addressed so that you can read and easily understand investment publications and can work successfully with investment advisers and sellers.

To that end, here are a few key terms and concepts. Only a few; this is a major field, and a small glossary here is no substitute for an appropriate dictionary, such as Brownstone and Franck's *Investor's Dictionary* (Van Nostrand Reinhold, 1981). Please note that many of these terms have been picked up and adapted from similar glossaries in two of my previous works, *The Manager's Lifelong Money Book* (with Jacques Sartisky, AMACOM, 1986) and *Personal Financial Survival* (with Jacques Sartisky, John Wiley, 1981).

Aggressive Growth Fund. See *Growth Investment*.

Annuity. A sum paid in equal installments over a period to recipients, called annuitants, under the terms of a bequest or an insurance policy, called an annuity policy.

Annuity policies come in different types and multiple options, but all such policies are purchased from an insurance company, which is contractually committed to pay the annuitant, owner, or beneficiary certain dollars at a time specified under the policy provisions. No matter what the type, the amounts paid by the insurer will never be greater than the cash values and interest accumulated in the contract. An annuity may be purchased either by specified periodic payments over a period of time before the date on which the company is obligated to begin payments, or by a lump sum of money to the insurance company, with the annuity payments to commence immediately or at a specified date thereafter.

During the accumulation period, an annuitant who has deferred receiving payments until some future date may, if desired, withdraw the accumulated cash values; if the annuitant dies, the beneficiary of the policy will receive the proceeds. However, once annuity payments have begun, the annuitant no longer has the right to withdraw those monies and they remain irrevocably in the hands of the insurance company; the company's only obligation then is to make periodic payments as stated in the contract.

Some companies offer *variable annuities;* the contract provisions are usually the same as for fixed annuities, but the periodic payments are variable, not fixed. The amount of the payment to the annuitant is determined by the success of a special investment account in which are placed the monies of owners of this type of policy, to be invested by the company. Such policies generally provide for a "floor," or basic minimum payment.

A *single-premium deferred annuity* has the basic elements of an "immediate annuity," but has some special characteristics. The deposit to the insurance company is not irrevocably given, but may be withdrawn by the owner of the policy at any time, partially or totally, before the date on which payments are to begin; in some contracts, this date can be as late as age 85 of the annuitant. The interest paid by the insurance company varies with the current interest rate, with a floor interest rate guaranteed in the contract. The interest is tax-deferred during the accumulation period, and upon withdrawal of funds, the annuitant or owner has no tax obligation until the sum withdrawn exceeds the sum initially deposited.

The contract thus allows for a fixed dollar deposit, interest payments at current rates with a rate floor guaranteed by the insurance company, and tax-deferred yield during accumulation. And, since the single-premium deferred annuity is an insurance contract, the proceeds are not subject to probate costs but on the death of the annuitant are paid directly to a named beneficiary. A variation, the *flexible premium retirement annuity*, is similar except that payments into the insurance contract may be made periodically rather than in a single lump sum.

Appreciation; Appreciation Potential. Appreciation is the extent to which an asset has gained in value, whether or not that value has been actually realized by selling the asset. "Appreciation potential" is investment-community jargon for "It may go up." Because this is a term used mainly by those with something to sell, there is—quite understandably—no opposite term, such as depreciation potential. For example, common stock is said to have appreciation potential when those trading it feel that, for any of several reasons, it may go up. If the rise in market prices is thought to be only for the near term, the stock is said to have short-term appreciation potential; if only for the long term, then long-term appreciation potential. Less pretentiously, a stock may be described as having either growth potential or its opposite, downside risk.

Asset-Backed Securities. Pools of investment money created by putting together large bodies of debt obligations and selling shares in the pool as securities are described as being asset-backed. They are also described as being *collateralized*, for it is the collateral behind them that distinguishes them from bare promises to pay. Those that are backed by mortgages are also often called *mortgage-backed securities*. As the essence of the transaction involved is that pooled promises to pay are passed through to securities purchasers, they are also called *pass-through securities*.

In this period, more kinds of asset-backed securities are being created, as lenders and securities sellers apply the principle of asset-backing to new kinds of debt obligations. As of this writing, federal agencies and many private sector lenders have created a considerable body of asset-backed securities, including Ginnie Maes (Government National Mortgage Association obligations); Fannie Maes (Federal National Mortgage Association obligations); Freddie Macs (Federal Home Loan Mortgage Association obligations); Sallie Maes (Student National Marketing Association obligations); Small Business Administration pooled obligations; pools of automobile loans; computer lease pools; and a wide range of private real estate loan pools.

A considerable number of asset-backed mutual funds, unit trusts, and limited partnerships have also been created, with more to come.

Average. In ordinary usage, an average is an arithmetic mean. In securities markets, an average reflects the value of a group of selected stocks, which are thought to be representative of their markets as a whole and therefore indicators of market health. Familiar examples are the Dow Jones Industrial, Standard & Poor's 500, and the New York Stock Exchange averages.

The Dow Jones averages are actually three different current

stock price averages, composed, respectively, of industrial, transportation, and utilities stocks. The best known and most frequently referred to is the industrial average, composed of 30 well-known common stocks. It is also by far the best known of all the stock market averages, and its fluctuations are watched closely by people who follow stock market price trends, even though the other major averages are composed of far larger numbers of stocks, fluctuate a good deal less, and are therefore somewhat more statistically reliable for predictive purposes.

Averaging. Averaging is a stock market investment technique also known as *dollar cost averaging*. It involves investing fixed sums of money in securities through periodic purchases, for example the monthly purchase of $1,000 in shares of a specific common stock over a period of six months. Short-term price fluctuations in that stock are ignored, on the theory that the long-term trend of that stock and indeed of the whole stock market is up, and that the purchase of sound stocks over the long term can only prove profitable.

Back Load. See *Load*.

Balanced Fund. A diversely invested mutual fund. From the start it is organized to invest in several kinds of stocks and bonds at the same time and to shift emphasis from one to another as fund managers' assessments of market situations change from time to time. Many mutual funds are not so organized. Instead they move from one kind of investment, such as municipal bonds or common stocks or even a single kind of common stock, to cash and cash instruments, without the ability to move relatively freely among an assortment of stocks and debt instruments.

Basis. In bond markets, basis means the rate of interest paid on bonds and other debt securities, expressed in points. One basis point is $1/100$ of 1%.

In stock analysis, it means the annual rate of return on stock, figuring the actual return as a proportion of the current market value of the stock.

Bear. See *Bull*.

Blue Chip. A synonym for high-quality investment, now applied widely to many noninvestment items and matters of value. Blue chip common stocks are the stocks of large, highly regarded companies, which have grown in value and paid dividends over a period measured in decades. They are therefore thought to be rather safe investments, with little chance of omitting dividends and losing value quickly and catastrophically.

Blind Pool. A pool of money gathered from investors before any significant investments have been made is quite properly called a blind pool. Investors are in that situation going in blind, relying upon the assurances and sometimes the track records of sellers and investment managers, rather than upon their own analyses of the specific investments involved. Blind pools are most often encountered in the limited partnership form of investment, as when general partners gather a pool of money they will then invest in certain kinds of properties. As a practical matter, startup mutual funds are also blind pools, for a few early transactions do not make a track record.

Boiler Room. Also called **Bucket Shop.** These two investment-industry slang terms mean the same thing—a fraudulent investment-selling firm. These are the kinds of illegal operations that give telephone selling a bad name. Their representatives sell mainly by telephone and will sell anything that is currently popular—as long as they can make a great deal of money doing it.

Bond. A tie that binds, and a word with a dozen different meanings and scores of uses. In finance, *bond* refers to a debt instrument issued by a corporation or government, in which the issuer promises to pay back the money borrowed from bond buyers, with interest, within a specified time. Usually, interest is payable in installments during the life of the debt obligation, and principal is repaid in a lump sum at the end of the period; sometimes, however, as in some government bonds, interest accretes during the debt period and is included with principal repayment at the end of the period. Bonds are usually medium- to long-term debt instruments, running five years or more.

Bond Fund. A mutual fund that limits its investments to either bonds or cash instruments, trading in bonds with the money invested in it.

A specific form of bond fund is the *municipal bond fund,* which limits its bond-trading activities to state and municipal bonds, thereby reaching for the tax advantages inherent in these kinds of debt obligations, which are usually exempt from federal taxes and sometimes from state and local taxes as well.

Bond Market. Bonds of all kinds are traded on many stock exchanges, but no exchange dominates the trading in bonds as the New York Stock Exchange dominates stock trading. Instead, bond trading proceeds over the counter, through a network of firms trading in these debt obligations; all of them together make up the bond market. Most bond transactions are very large and represent trades between financial instititions, such as banks, pension funds, mutual funds, and insurance companies, buying and selling for their own accounts.

Book Value. This is an accounting concept, and a valuable one when trying to assess the intrinsic asset value of a business or a share of common stock. It is calculated a little differently for each. For a business, book value is the difference between all assets and all liabilities; putting it a little differently, it is the net of assets minus liabilities. Those assets are valued as part of a going business, rather than at their scrap or salvage value, which would be much less; and that is proper, for it is that going business that is being evaluated.

When the intrinsic value of a share of common stock is being assessed, any preferred stock outstanding must also be taken into account. To estimate a stock's book value, you would take the net of the company's assets minus liabilities, subtract the value of any preferred stock outstanding, and divide the resulting net by the number of outstanding shares of common stock. The result is the book value. For example, if assets were $100 and liabilities $50, the net would be $50. If preferred stock worth $10 were subtracted from that $50, the result would be $40. If there were 40 common stock shares outstanding, their book value would be $1 per share.

This is an important figure. If stock is selling below its book value, the company may be in terrible trouble, perhaps in the process of being forced out of business, with the resulting reevaluation of assets way down to salvage value. Or the company may be far undervalued and thus a very good buy and a prime takeover candidate. Conversely, if a stock is selling far above its book value, it may be a company with interesting growth and profit possibilities that has shown extraordinary results and that may soon show more. Or it may be a company that is far overvalued, as were so many "glamour" stocks in the 1960s, and thus a very bad buy.

Bucket Shop. See *Boiler Room*.

Bull; Bear. These traditional stock market terms have now moved out into the general language as synonyms for *optimist* and *pessimist*. In the financial world, a bull thinks a specific stock or debt obligation, or a whole market or set of markets, is likely to go up, and buys now in anticipation of that rise. Bulls often buy on margin (that is, on borrowed money) and hold the securities or commodities in brokers' margin accounts in an attempt to maximize the impact of their investments, holding on as long as possible in a falling market.

A bear thinks that a single investment or group of investments will go down, and sells rather than buys. While bulls often buy long and hold, bears often do the opposite; they sell short—that is, they sell stocks they do not yet own, planning and hoping to cover their sales by buying stocks later at lower prices, profiting from the difference between the two sets of prices.

Capital Gains. The profits resulting from sale of an asset. For example, when securities or realty worth $10,000 is sold later for $15,000, the difference of $5,000 may be capital gain—and therefore taxable, for that is the main significance of the concept.

Capital Stock. Collectively, all the stock representing ownership of a corporation, including common and preferred stock. It is all the stock held by the public and all that has been issued and is owned by the corporation itself, as when stock has been sold to the public and then repurchased by the corporation.

The underlying or intrinsic value of the total capital stock of a corporation is its book value, or the net of all assets minus all liabilities. That net is one measure of the total equity in the corporation. Another measure is often supplied by the market value placed on publicly traded stock of that corporation.

Certificate of Deposit. A document evidencing a deposit in a bank, issued by a bank to the owner of the deposit; a passbook is the same kind of instrument, in a different physical form.

They are commonly called CDs and occur in two basic forms. One form, widely sold by commerical banks to individuals, is a demand certificate of deposit, which specifies that the depositor can withdraw the deposit on demand, although suffering substantial interest-rate penalties for premature withdrawal. Because of its demand nature, this kind of certificate of deposit is not tradable in investment markets.

The second form is a time certificate of deposit, payable at some specified future time. Such certificates are widely traded in money markets, as they are usually direct obligations of highly regarded banks, although not as safe as direct federal debt obligations.

Some time certificates of deposit are issued in denominations so high that they are outside the normal buying range of all but the wealthiest individuals. But individuals can reach them—and their sometimes attractive rates—through mutual funds, notably money market funds, which routinely include them in their portfolios.

Chartist. See *Fundamentalist.*

Closed-End Fund. See *Mutual Funds.*

Collateral. Something of value used as security for a loan. Normal collateral consists of property of determinable value that belongs to the borrower or to someone guaranteeing the loan for the borrower, which on default will become the property of the lender. When a lender and borrower enter into a mortgage loan, the property itself is collateral for the loan. When a borrower formally pledges any property, such as stocks and other financial instruments, as security for a loan, that which is pledged is collateral. When a borrower gives the lender physical possession of property so pledged, to be returned on repayment of the loan, the loan is called a *collateral loan.*

Collateralized Securities. See *Asset-Backed Securities.*

Commercial Paper. In the widest sense, this term includes all short-term debt instruments issued by businesses of all kinds. Such notes are negotiable and may be traded and used as collateral. Some are traded widely, are rated for safety, and have become part of the money market. These are the instruments issued by major businesses, which stand behind them, essentially as they do for any unsecured longer-term instrument, such as a bond, with their full faith and credit, which is a promise to pay. The instruments are as good as the businesses issuing them, which in the case of a healthy major company may be very good indeed and in the case of a troubled company not very good at all.

Because the instruments are normally issued in very large denominations, from $100,000 to $1,000,000, very few individuals can trade in them. However, money market mutual funds do, and that is the way individuals can reach for their yields, which are higher than, though generally not quite as safe as, federally issued and federally insured debt obligations.

Common Stock. An unrestricted ownership share in a corporation, the kind of stock that is normally traded in investment markets. Common stock is by far the main form such ownership shares take. The owner shares fully in risks and opportunities and votes its proportion of ownership in the issuing corporation. The owner of preferred stock, by contrast, may share less risk but also shares in opportunities to only a limited degree. When a stock is reported as rising or falling in market value, it is a common stock that is being described, unless otherwise noted.

Convertible. Some bonds and preferred stocks carry the privilege of conversion over to a stated number of shares of common stock at a stated price within a stated period after issue. Their purchasers can either hold these convertibles in their purchased form until maturity, or exercise the privilege of converting them, depending upon whether or not the stated amount of common stock is worth more than the bond or preferred stock.

Cyclical Stocks. These are the traded stocks of companies thought to be quickly affected by the ups and downs of the economy. Their prices therefore fluctuate more directly than most stocks, as the business cycle moves between prosperity and depression or recession. For example, companies manufacturing consumer goods and therefore depending wholly or largely on discretionary consumer purchases, such as automobiles, furniture, and appliances, may feel the impact of a recession very sharply; of course they are also the beneficiaries of pent-up demand as a period of prosperity unfolds.

Debt Obligation. Any financial instrument evidencing a measurable debt, such as a bond, bill, or note.

Distribution Fee. See *Load*.

Dollar Cost Averaging. See *Averaging*.

Early Withdrawal. Also called **Premature Withdrawal.** Any withdrawal of funds from an account that results in interest or tax penalties is called an early or premature withdrawal. For example, taking out part of your IRA funds before the legal age of withdrawal is reached (currently 59½ years), is premature, and results in tax penalty. Similarly, a withdrawal of funds from a CD before the full term of the CD is reached will result in an interest penalty, and is also called early or premature.

Earnings per Share. Earnings are profits. Earnings per share, a very important indicator of the economic health of an enterprise, are profits minus taxes and preferred stock dividends (both of which have to be paid first), divided by the number of shares of common stock outstanding. For example, if earnings are $1,000 and taxes are $400, net after-tax earnings are $600. If preferred stock dividends totaling $100 are subtracted, and if there are 500 common shares outstanding, net earnings per share are $1 each. In investment publications, you will sometimes see the abbreviaton EPS.

Fannie Maes. The debt obligations of the Federal National Mortgage Association. See also *Asset-Backed Securities*.

Federal Agency Issues. The debt obligations of several federal agencies and federally related organizations are collectively called federal agency issues. These include the Small Business Administration and the Government National Mortgage Association, which are federal agencies, as well as the Federal National Mortgage Association, the Student National Marketing Association, and the Federal Home Loan Mortgage Association, which are federally related but not federal agencies. These do not include the debt obligations of the U.S. Treasury which are collectively called *Treasuries* or *Treasury issues*.

Flexible-Premium Deferred Annuity. See *Annuity*.

Freddie Macs. The debt obligations of the Federal Home Loan Mortgage Association. See also *Asset-Backed Securities*.

Front Load. See *Load*.

Fundamentalist; Chartist. The market prices of securities fluctuate, and a whole industry has been built around attempts to predict the future course of those fluctuations. Securities analysts, investment advisers, and market forecasting services all claim expert knowledge, advise, predict, hedge their claims and bets, and seek the fruits of successful prediction—or at least seek to be recognized by investors as successful forecasters. There are two major schools of thought, and several variations, on how to approach forecasting.

One major approach is that of the *fundamentalists*, who believe that basic economic, social, and political trends plus specific company facts must be understood and assessed on the way toward successful prediction. They want to know a great deal about specific company managements, balance sheets, cash flow statements, industry trends, and national and international factors that may have an impact—in short, all the facts underlying an investment.

Another major approach is that of the *chartists*, many of whom want to know very little about those things that concern the fundamentalists. Chartists want to know how a graph showing the past performance of a market or group of investments can be used to predict the future course of price fluctuation in those investments.

As is usually true, seeming polar opposites are often only tendencies. Most fundamentalists will also study charts of previous price movements, while continuing to ask basic economic questions. Chartists also—though many are purists—will ask basic questions, while focusing on their charts.

Fund of Funds. A mutual fund organized solely to invest in the shares of other mutual funds. The form emerged in the boom years of the 1960s and gave fund promoters an opportunity to add additional layers of fees to existing fees. It has reemerged to a limited extent in the 1980s.

General Partnership. See *Limited Partnership*.

Ginnie Maes. The debt obligations of the Government National Mortgage Association. See also *Asset-Backed Securities*.

Ginnie Mae Funds. Also called **Government Plus Funds.** Bond mutual funds in which all debt obligations held by the fund are federally guaranteed are called Ginnie Mae funds, or Government Plus funds. In this period, when Ginnie Maes have been very attractive to investors, their promoters have tended to call them Ginnie Mae funds. See also *Asset-Backed Securities*.

Glamour Stocks. "Hot" stocks, "glamour" stocks, stocks that "everybody is buying and you can't miss on"—these are the stocks that dreams are made of. That is not reality, however; reality is a glamour stock that has lost its glamour just after you have bought it at an inflated price. Glamour stocks are those that are extremely popular for a time, far more so than is usually justified by performance or prospects. Basically they go up because more and more people are buying them in hope of quick profits. Often that hope of profit is spurred by a real, though temporary, surge or an anticipated surge in profits, as was true of some gambling stocks in the late 1970s. Sometimes a new technology that seems to offer enormous profit potential spurs popularity, as in some computer and electronic stocks in the 1960s.

Gold Shares. Stocks representing ownership shares in companies that are mainly in the gold mining business. During times of historic run-ups in the world price of gold, they are often enormously popular, since their profits considerably reflect the rising price of gold, even though they are highly speculative investments.

Growth and Income Fund. A mutual fund that invests in common stocks for both growth and dividends, and is therefore normally somewhat more conservatively managed than funds aiming almost entirely at quick growth in market values.

Growth Fund. See *Growth Investment*.

Growth Investment. Any that is oriented primarily toward securing growth in the value of the investment itself, rather than immediate financial return.

The concept is often encountered in stock trading, when a company is described as a *growth company,* meaning one that is experiencing rapid growth in net asset value, in sales, and often in total ownership equity as the value of its stock appreciates (that stock is then called a *growth stock).* However, such stocks rarely pay much in the way of dividends, since much of what might otherwise be profits and dividends is being plowed back into the company to spur future growth.

Growth funds and *aggressive growth funds* (often quite properly also called *high-risk funds)* are sometimes also popular. These are mutual funds focusing on growth stocks and looking for rapid appreciation in total fund asset value, rather than for income to be passed along to fund participants. Similarly, there are *growth portfolios,* individual investment portfolios geared to the acquisition of growth stocks.

Hot Money. In the financial world, this is investment money, usually large amounts of it, that moves from investment vehicle to investment vehicle, and from country to country, in search of the highest possible rate of return. It is speculating money, and may one week be found in currency trading, the next week in gold, and the week after that in commodity futures. It is most emphatically *not* to be followed on its adventurous way; small investors who speculate almost inevitably find themselves buying too late to buy low and selling too late to make a profit or even to avoid a substantial loss.

Hot Stock. See *Glamour Stock*.

Income Fund. Mutual funds aimed primarily at securing current income for their participants, which therefore focus on securities yielding cash payout rather than growth. They are far from recession-proof, but they tend to be somewhat recession-resistant, for companies consistently paying substantial dividends over a long period tend to be some of the most stable and best-regarded current "blue chips." Of course, yesterday's blue chip can become today's troubled company, but it is the business of fund managers to watch fund investments, so these stocks will probably not be kept in the fund too long.

In recent years, many highly speculative limited partnerships have also been called income funds by their promoters and sellers. Therefore, those looking at anything labled "income funds" should very carefully explore what it really is before making buying decisions.

Junk Bonds. These are high-risk, high-interest, low-rated bonds sold by some brokers as good speculative opportunities, on the theory that while some few may fail, the majority will not, and the interest rates paid will more than make up for the individual bond losses. A questionable theory, and a game for professionals, if anyone.

Listed; Unlisted. In order to be *listed* on an organized stock exchange, and therefore traded on that exchange, a stock must meet the exchange's rules for size and financial condition of the issuing company and the number of shares outstanding and tradable. By far the majority of publicly owned stocks are traded in over-the-counter markets, that is, directly between brokers rather than through the medium of an organized stock exchange. Such stocks are *unlisted*, and they include many well-known and highly respected American companies.

Load. In finance and insurance, a load is a sales charge. The term is sometimes used widely to include all sales charges and commissions, but is usually applied to sales charges on mutual fund and life insurance and annuity purchases. Many mutual fund and some life insurance annuity purchases do not have sales charges attached to them. They are called *no-load* funds and policies. That is a competitive selling matter, especially in the mutual funds industry, where for many years most large funds had substantial sales charges but found themselves competing with smaller funds that did not. Although the trend is away from such sales charges, they still exist and should be noted when considering purchase of a mutual fund.

Some investments and insurance contracts do not have *front-load charges* (payable on entering the fund), but may have *back-load charges* (payable on leaving the fund) or expense factors that are beyond the norm and act as a load, which are usually called *distribution fees*.

Some mutual funds carrying sales charges somewhat lower than the highest going rates are called *low-load funds*.

Low Load. See *Load*.

Market. Speaking broadly, a market is an arena within which valuables are traded. That can include retail stores, bazaars, organized and over-the-counter stock markets, and worldwide commodities and currencies markets. Rather confusingly, all those involved as specialists in specific markets refer to their own area of interest as "the market," much as those deeply involved in a particular line of work invariably refer to their own fields as "the business."

"How did the market do today?" is a question widely encountered among brokers and investors. It is usually answered, "It went up (or down) X points." In that instance, the market referred to is almost always the New York Stock Exchange, and the "it" that went up or down is the Dow Jones Industrial Average, the most widely followed and quoted American index of stock prices.

Money Market; Money Market Fund. Institutions and monied individuals all over the world trade in short-term debt obligations, such as the U.S. government's Treasury bills, bank certificates of deposit, and commerical paper of all kinds. The sum of all those who trade and their trades is the world money market, which is really a series of interlocked markets operating simultaneously in many countries.

As many of the obligations traded are issued in denominations of $100,000 and up, most individuals were, until recent years, effectively barred from participation in these markets, even though many of the obligations traded were and are attractive investment opportunities. In the past decade, however, the growing popularity of money market funds, which are mutual funds organized to invest in these and similar instruments, have made them accessible to smaller investors—who have flocked to them, especially under conditions of high short-term interest rates and otherwise unstable financial markets.

Mortgage-Backed Securities. See *Asset-Backed Securities*.

Municipal Bond. The word *municipal* is somewhat misleading here. Municipalities are units of government smaller than counties, usually cities and towns. Municipal bonds, however, include all government debt obligations other than those of the federal government, including county and state obligations. See also *Bond Fund*.

Mutual Funds. All mutual funds embody the same concept: by pooling their funds and paying professional fund managers, small investors can profit from their investments and simultaneously diversify those investments far better than they could alone. Any mutual fund, however invested, is a pool of investors' money; investors buy shares and may or may not pay sales charges.

A fund may consist of a limited number of shares, in which case it is called a *closed-end fund*, or it may be as large as the number of shares it succeeds in selling to the public, in which case it is called an *open-end fund*. Investors in open-end funds can sell their shares back to the fund at any time, which is called *redemption*. Closed-end funds are sold on the over-the-counter market, much like stocks.

Mutual fund pools of investment money can focus on many kinds of investments, including money market instruments, several kinds of stocks, and bonds; they can specialize in one kind of investment or attempt to balance among several.

No-Load. See *Load*.

Odd Lots; Round Lots. Stocks traded in anything other than even hundred-share lots and their multiples are called *odd lots*, while lots of hundred-unit multiples are called *round lots*. The distinction is significant for small investors, as trades of small numbers of shares have traditionally cost considerably more per share than larger trades.

Open-End Fund. See *Mutual Funds*.

Paper Gains. See *Realize*.

Par Value. The value printed on the face of an instrument; sometimes called *face value*. Common stocks are usually issued with a face value far less than market value, to minimize documentary taxes paid on such instruments. For preferred stocks and bonds, that par value is very close to market value at time of issuance, with trading markets then setting fluctuating market prices. For negotiable instruments, such as checks, par value is the value of the instrument before such subtractions as discounts and handling charges.

Pass-Through Securities. See *Asset-Backed Securities*.

Portfolio. A portfolio is a container; an investment portfolio is a bag of investments of a single owner, whether that owner is an individual or an organization, and whether the portfolio is self-managed or in the hands of a professional investment manager. The word may be used to describe all investments of every kind held, including stocks, bonds, real estate investments, and even savings; more often it is used to describe a body of tradable investments.

Preferred Stock. A form of ownership share issued by a corporation, which is literally preferred over common stock in issuance of dividends, which must be distributed to preferred shareholders before common shareholders. It sometimes also carries a preferred position in voting on some corporate affairs.

Preferred stock dividend amounts are specified by the terms of original issue; they may be *cumulative* (payable in subsequent years if not paid in a given year or years) or *noncumulative* (if a dividend is *passed*, or not paid, in a given year, it is lost). Some preferred stocks can, to a limited extent, share profits beyond stated dividends with common stocks, which have neither guarantees nor limits placed on their shares of profit participation,.

Premium. Generally, "something more." For example, when a lender demands more than the interest stated in a mortgage loan instrument, when additional "points" of interest are paid at the start of the mortgage repayment period, or when a seller demands a price somewhat higher than normal because of the allegedly higher quality of goods or services.

In the financial industries, the word has other related, but somewhat different, meanings. The market price at which a commodity option sells is called a premium. The amount at which a security or commodity is selling above its face value is called its premium. The amount at which a new stock issue is selling above its issue price is called its premium, even though its issuing price normally has nothing at all to do with its face, or par, value. In insurance, the payments made on an insurance policy are called premiums.

Realize. In financial terms, to realize is to turn something of value into something else of value, usually cash. It is usually used in connection with appreciation in value. You can realize a loss on a transaction, but most people speak of a loss as being taken, while gain is realized, or money is made. Until gains are realized, they are *paper gains*, although paper gains do have increased real value as collateral.

Reinvestment. Placing proceeds or profits from one investment back into more of the same or some other investment.

It is important not to reinvest blindly. It is quite natural for a securities salesperson, for example, to assume that you will invest stock sales proceeds in more stock, but that should not be your assumption. At the point at which you have made any investment liquid (turned it into cash), all options are once again open, and you should freshly examine them.

Sallie Maes. The debt obligations of the Student National Marketing Association. See also *Asset-Backed Securities*.

Sector Fund. The 1980s term for mutual funds organized to appeal to particular kinds of investing interests. In the 1960s and 1970s they were generally called *special interest funds*. The "sector" referred to in this period is most likely to be a sector of an economy, consisting of one or more industries, or a sector of the world, consisting of a geographical region.

Single-Premium Deferred Annuity. See *Annuity*.

Special Interest Fund. See *Sector Fund*.

Special Situation. As a stock market term, this characterizes a security considered to have unusual profit possibilities. For example, a stock that is selling for considerably less than its underlying asset value may be thought of as ready for a rebound because of impending profitable operations or because another company is about to purchase it at a per-share price far higher than its current market price. A company that is losing money may be under new management and be ready to be "turned around," with consequent increases in the market price of its stock.

It should be noted that most situations so assessed are not so special. Acquisition plans can fall through; new management may prove as unable as old management to solve intractable long-term problems. There is no simple measuring device with which you can separate truly special situations from quite ordinary, usually losing situations. Special situations are therefore properly regarded as speculations and should be treated with extreme skepticism.

Stock. See *Common Stock* and *Preferred Stock*.

Tax Shelter. Quite literally, investment vehicles designed to shelter income from taxation. They are means of securing greatly accelerated growth through the avoidance of taxes on current income and the consequent ability to reinvest and compound far greater pre-tax sums than would be possible from the investment of after-tax income. IRAs, pension and profit-sharing plans, and most municipals are major examples.

Treasury Issues; Treasuries. The debt obligations of the U.S. Treasury, including all Treasury bills, notes, and bonds, are collectively called Treasury issues, or simply Treasuries.

Unit Trust. A pool of specific debt obligations, such as specific corporate bonds, repackaged in small segments for sale to investors. A unit trust that uses a pool of specific municipals would be a *tax-exempt unit trust*.

Unlisted. See *Listed*.

Variable Annuity. See *Annuity*.

Yield. Yield is synonymous with rate of return. It is the actual return, as when a bond pays an interest rate of 8%, compared with the price originally paid for that bond. It is the rate of return, therefore, on the money invested, not bearing any relationship to any later value of the investment.

The *true yield* is the amount of interest received as related to the market value of the investment instrument; the amount received remains constant in dollars but the true yield expressed as a percentage changes in direct proportion to the market value of the underlying instrument.

Zero-Coupon Bond. In this recent and very popular bond form, dealers buy bonds from issuers, strip the future periodic interest payments from the bonds, to be sold separately, and sell the resulting bond instruments, which are then available at prices that seem very low, compared to the full face values the bonds will pay at maturity, many years later. These bonds are extremely sensitive to interest rate swings. Should interest rates go up and stay up, bond values will sharply decline. Should interest rates go down sharply, considerable gains in value may result, if established markets for the bonds exist.

Index

adjusted gross income, and IRA tax deductions, 24
aggressive growth funds, 114–116
annuities, 91–95
  deferred, 92
asset-backed securities, 55, 71–77

back load charges, 100–101
  of annuities, 93–94
balanced funds, 117, 135, 143
Bank of America, 76
bankruptcy, 29–30
Barron's, 12
basis points, 63, 74–75
blue chip stocks, 90
bond markets, 54
bond mutual funds, costs and risks of, 57
bonds, 6, 47–70
  asset-backed securities as, 74
  callable, 51
  convertible, 67
  debenture, 65
  federal, 53–55
  federal agency, 55–59
  revenue, 62
  savings, 55
  see also corporate bonds
borrowed money, *see* leverage
brokerage firms, 84–85, 139
Business Information Sources (Daniell), 13

callable bonds, 51
capital gains tax, 22
certificates of deposit (CD), 33, 35–46, 132, 134, 137
  incentives for purchasing, 40
  maturity dates of, 45
  money market funds vs., 112

penalties for early sale of, 43–44
  risk and yield of, 5
  term for, 42–45
closed-end mutual funds, 107–108
collateral
  of bonds, 51
  certificate of deposit as, 44
  for corporate bonds, 66
  IRA as, 136
collectibles, 31
commodity options, 6
common stock, 81–82
company pension plans, *see* pension plans
computerized trading, 89
convertible bonds, 67
corporate bonds, 49, 63–68
  fluctuation of, 65
  risk of, 5
costs
  of annuities, 93–94
  of moving money, 113
  of mutual funds, 97–103
  of trading stock, 84–87
Cote, Grant *(Directory of Business and Financial Services)*, 13
coupons, 54

Daniell, Lorna *(Business Information Sources)*, 13
databases, 13–14
debenture bond, 65
deferred annuity, 92
Directory of Business and Financial Services (Grant Cote), 13
discount brokers, 84–85, 139
distribution fees, 101–102
diversification, 104–106
Dow Jones Industrial Average, 79–80